A Cook's Compendium

OF **250** ESSENTIAL TIPS, TECHNIQUES, TRADE SECRETS & TASTY RECIPES

Jenni Davis

NEW
BURLINGTON
BOOKS

A QUARTO BOOK

Published in 2014 by
New Burlington Books
6 Blundell Street
London N7 9BH

ISBN: 978-0-85762-128-3

Conceived, designed and produced by
Quarto Publishing plc
The Old Brewery
6 Blundell Street
London
N7 9BH

QUAR.TTCS

Senior editor: Katie Crous
Copy editor: Philippa Kennard
Designer: John Grain
Design assistant: Martina Calvio
Photographer: Simon Pask
Home economist: Rob Watson
Picture researcher: Sarah Bell
Art director: Caroline Guest

Creative director: Moira Clinch
Publisher: Paul Carslake

Colour separation by PICA Digital Pte
Ltd, Singapore

Printed in China by 1010 Printing
International Ltd

10 9 8 7 6 5 4 3 2 1

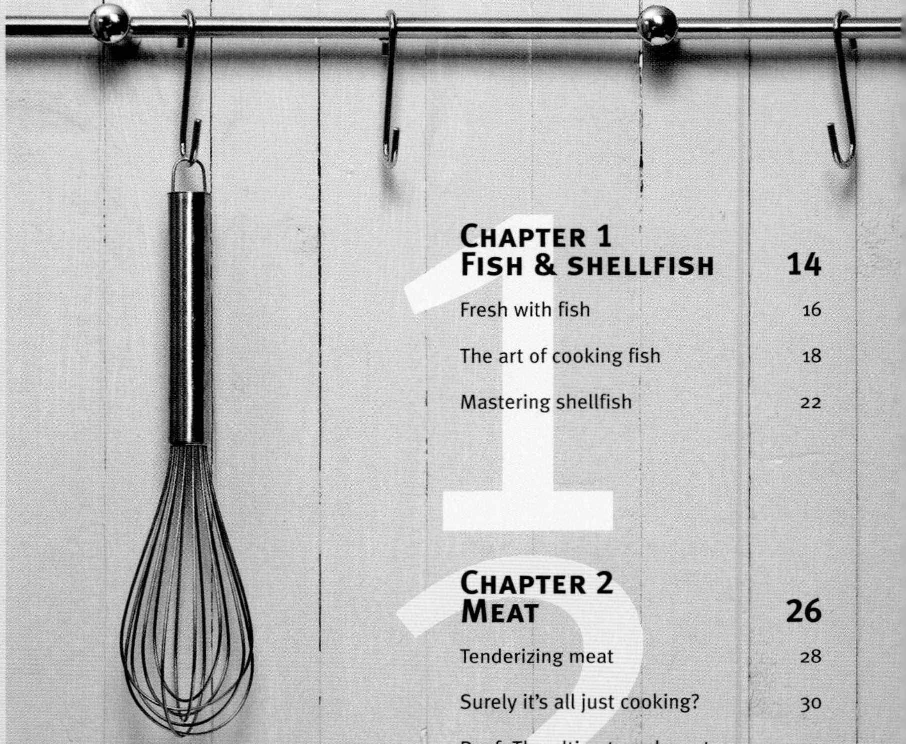

Contents

A Cook's
Compendium

Cooking is a joy. Not assembling packages and jars of processed foods and uniting them, but real cooking, from scratch, using the best ingredients. It's only when you serve your first batch of homemade pasta with a sauce of your own making, when a cube of tender meat falls apart almost before your fork reaches it, when the aroma of baking fills the kitchen, that you really start to understand why chefs love their work so much.

Cooking engages all your senses, often without you noticing. Taste is only part of it — you use your eyes to judge colour, your ears to listen for a sizzle, your nose to gauge progress. You touch steak, fish, a cake to assess whether it's cooked. Your intuition tells you what will work, and what won't. And these are just examples. Be aware of all your senses as you cook and you'll find it's as soothing as a meditation.

This isn't a recipe book, although there are recipes scattered throughout to demonstrate techniques. Rather, it's a book about 'how' and 'why' — cooking is a far less daunting prospect if you're armed with knowledge about how ingredients behave and why you don't always get the result you'd hoped for. From now on, you always will!

Jenni Davis

About this book

This book is organized into seven chapters — six of which represent a major food group. In each chapter you'll find recurring features that guide you seamlessly through the treasure trove of culinary secrets and tips stored within.

5 Reasons
Cupboard, refrigerator and freezer staples are highlighted, letting you know what you should have on hand and why.

Recipes
Access classic, sumptuous recipes from around the globe in simple, easy-to-follow instructions. Ingredients listed are for four people, unless stated otherwise.

Flavour combos
Take your recipes to another level with this quick visual guide that lets you see at a glance some unusual but perfectly matched ingredient combinations.

3 Golden rules
The essential dos and don'ts all culinary experts need to know.

'Try it' and 'Fix it'
Regular panels introduce you to clever gadgets and ingenious ideas for tackling certain foods and common problems you might encounter in your kitchen.

Step-by-step sequences
Photographic steps show you exactly what to do to achieve the best results from key culinary techniques.

Key ingredients

Filling an empty kitchen can be daunting! However, to be a culinary whizz, you need only a few staple items stored correctly, so that they are always on hand.

The really useful items

Here, we take a look at the five most useful items to keep in your refrigerator, your freezer and your cupboard, with a few extras to guarantee you'll always be able to conjure up something with the wow factor.

The freezer

What?	How?	Why?	For how long?
Homemade ragù	One-meal portions in airtight freezer bags or containers	See page 61	Up to 3 months
Chicken breasts	Individually wrapped	See page 47	Up to 4 months
Puff pastry sheets	Manufacturer's packaging; once opened, wrap unused sheets in aluminium foil	See page 135	Up to 1 year
Petits pois	Manufacturer's packaging; once opened, reseal the package or fold the top and secure with a freezer bag clip or clothes peg	See page 84	Up to 1 year
Spinach nuggets	As for petits pois	See page 87	Up to 1 year

The cupboard

What?	How?	Why?	For how long?
Risotto rice	Store in an airtight container once opened	See page 54	1 year
Penne pasta	As for risotto rice	See page 58	1 year
Polenta	As for risotto rice	See page 68	1 year
Tinned beans	Store leftovers in a covered container in the refrigerator	See page 72	Once opened, use within 2 days
Tinned tuna	As for beans	See page 16	Once opened, use within 2 days

The fridge

What?	How?	Why?	For how long?
Butter	Manufacturer's wrapper	See page 127	3 weeks
Eggs	Egg carton	See page 112	2 weeks
Pancetta	Manufacturer's packaging; once opened, wrap in waxed paper and store in a container	See page 39	3 weeks
Hard cheese	Wrap in waxed paper, then cover with aluminium foil	See page 120	Up to 1 month
Lemons	Sealed plastic bag	See page 93	Up to 1 month

Rotate!

Keeping the number of items you store to a manageable minimum helps avoid waste and confusion, but you still need to be vigilant about rotating food in the refrigerator (dried, tinned and frozen goods last a lot longer but still need to be used eventually). Dull as it sounds, there's much to be said for planning ahead for, say, a week. That way, you can organize your daily menus to include any chilled items that need using up, and replace them when you next shop.

Freezer burn

Items stored in the freezer need to be carefully packed to avoid freezer burn, which occurs when the food is exposed to air. Freezer-burned food is still edible, but that's the best that can be said for it — the flavour, texture and nutrients will be lost. Plastic containers with airtight snap-on lids are ideal for storing homemade dishes such as ragù, but if you don't want to use plastic, open-freeze the food in a foil-lined container, then lift out and wrap in foil. Screw-top Kilner jars with an airtight seal are also freezer proof. Fold opened packages to remove as much of the air inside as possible, then seal the bag with a clip or clothes peg.

An eclectic collection
Airtight tins and jars can look enticing and keep cupboard ingredients fresh. Warning: Pasta in a jar without a lid is for decorative purposes only!

Umami: The fifth taste

Savoury food falls into two categories: the sort that leaves you vaguely dissatisfied, and the sort with 'umami'. In the early 20th century, a Japanese chemistry professor, Kikunae Ikeda, identified a particularly appealing taste common to certain foods. It didn't fall into any of the recognized taste categories — sweet, sour, bitter, salty — but had its own intensely savoury character, which came to be known as *umami*, the 'fifth taste'. Store naturally umami-rich items in your kitchen to make your taste buds really happy.

Anchovies These tiny fish melt away into nothingness when cooked, leaving no fishy taste or texture but plenty of umami. **Serve with:** Add an anchovy to any meat-based dish, such as ragù (see page 61), at the start of cooking, and to marinades and dressings. **Golden rules:** Anchovy is a common allergen, so alert guests when you use it. Preserved anchovies tend to be very salty, so allow for this when seasoning your dish.

Dried mushrooms (porcini or ceps) Like anchovies, dried mushrooms almost disappear when cooked but are umami-rich. **Serve with:** Add to slow-cooked meat dishes (no need to rehydrate) and risottos (rehydrate in boiling water for 20 minutes or so). **Golden rule:** Save the soaking liquid, which will be full of flavour — remove the mushrooms with a slotted spoon, then pass the liquid through a fine sieve lined with muslin.

Tomato paste Tomatoes were one of the original food items that inspired the discovery of umami. **Serve with:** Any tomato-based sauce for added richness and depth of flavour. **Golden rule:** With tomato paste, the flavour is intensified, so a little goes a lot further than fresh or tinned tomatoes, subtly supporting the dish rather than hogging the limelight.

Garlic This wonderful little bulb packed with individual cloves that are full of flavour is a great source of umami. **Serve with:** Use in dips and sauces, and add to butter or oil when pan-frying or roasting fish, meat or vegetables. Garlic butter is divine! **Golden rules:** Roasting garlic mellows out its flavour and makes it less aggressive (see page 99). Look out for fermented 'black' garlic, which is sweet, sticky and yummy.

Extra virgin olive oil A good-quality, cold-pressed extra virgin olive oil is so full of umami you could drink it on its own! **Serve with:** Alternatively, you could use it in dressings, as a drizzle or simply for dunking sourdough bread (see page 139). **Golden rule:** Extra virgin olive oil comes from the first pressing of the olives; the 'standard' olive oil made from subsequent pressings is fine for cooking unless a recipe specifies otherwise.

Parmesan Considered by many to be the height of umami heaven, Parmesan is irresistibly salty, but there's definitely something more, a subtle undertone. **Serve with:** Works brilliantly with tomato-based sauces, and a generous tablespoon, freshly grated, takes a simple bowl of pasta or risotto from bland to sublime. **Golden rule:** If adding to soup, stock or sauce as it cooks, remember to adjust the seasoning.

Black olives Meaty, satisfying and with a distinctive flavour, olives are either loved or hated. **Serve with:** A black olive tapenade, made with anchovies, adds a double dose of umami to meat or fish dishes. **Golden rule:** They're worth learning to love if you don't already!

Asparagus Obviously not a cupboard staple, it's included because, like tomatoes, asparagus drew the attention of the Japanese professor Kikunae Ikeda. **Serve with:** Melted butter. A few stalks added to a simple omelette or risotto will lift the dish to deliciousness. Use trimmings to flavour stock. **Golden rule:** Buy it in season to enjoy it fresh from the soil.

Balsamic vinegar A rich, dark, syrupy vinegar made from reduced unfermented grape juice. **Serve with:** Marries wonderfully with fruit and also works well in desserts — if you're out to impress, try serving strawberries with a balsamic zabaglione (see page 119). **Golden rule:** Invest in one aged slowly in wooden barrels — the best has the perfect balance of sweetness and acidity, and adds umami to marinades and dressings.

Wine vinegar (red and white) Wine vinegar is produced by the natural fermentation of wine. **Serve with:** Use in dressings and marinades, and to add the 'sour' element in sweet-and-sour dishes. White wine vinegar is a key ingredient in beurre blanc (see page 126), which adds an umami kick to seafood. **Golden rule:** Invest in one aged for several months in wooden barrels.

IMPROMPTU UMAMI MEALS

Just a hint of umami flavour added to everyday foods turns them into something sublime — no special shopping trip required.

Oil   eggs   pancetta

spinach   Parmesan   garlic

 FRITATTA

Risotto rice   dried mushrooms   chicken

spinach   garlic

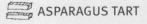 RISOTTO

Puff pastry   asparagus   anchovies

hard cheese   black olives

 ASPARAGUS TART

Penne   red kidney beans   tuna

petits pois   black olives

 ONE-PAN DINNER

FIX IT

The sharp edge A kitchen knife goes blunt very quickly, so it's good practice to sharpen your knife every time you use it. If you've invested in a really good knife, it's worth investing in a ceramic sharpening steel as well. A less expensive alternative is a traditional ridged honing steel, the type often supplied with a set of knives. A butcher or professional chef sharpens knives at a mesmerizing speed. You'll need to take it slower at first! The important thing to remember is to maintain a 12°–20° angle as you draw the knife along the steel.

Kitchen knife · Flexible knife · Small serrated knife · Cook's knife · Bread knife

1 Hold the steel in your left hand (or right, if you're left-handed), making sure it feels secure and comfortable. You can rest the tip of the steel on a firm surface until you gain confidence. Hold the knife in your other hand. Rest the heel of the blade (the end nearest the handle) against the base of the steel.

2 Maintaining the 12°–20° angle, draw the blade along the steel, at the same time drawing your hand out to the side so that the whole length of the blade is exposed to the steel. The hand holding the steel stays still. The midpoints of the blade and the steel should meet at the same time.

3 Continue until the tip of the knife meets the tip of the steel. Repeat the process, this time with the knife on the underside of the steel. Continue until the blade is sharp. Always remember that a sharp knife is a serious kitchen hazard so you should be careful when using and storing it.

Utensils, gadgets and gizmos

It's easy to spend a fortune on kitchen gadgetry, but is it necessary and will it make life easier? In some cases, yes — and in most cases, no. Those items of kitchenware that you really can't do without are worth the investment, however, as they'll last you a lifetime. Basically, all you need is a really, really sharp knife and a solid pot ...!

The knife

Choosing a knife is like choosing a mattress — different people have different needs. When selecting this essential implement, pay attention to its brand name. Aim to buy from a well-known and respected manufacturer. Kitchen knives are traditionally made of steel, and as long as you sharpen your knife regularly and correctly, good-quality steel is still your best bet.

Unless you intend to take your butchery skills to an advanced level, an all-purpose cook's knife will serve most of your food preparation needs. The cook's knife comes in three sizes, so select the one that will best suit your culinary tastes. Before making your purchase, hold the knife as you would when using it, to check that it feels balanced and the handle is comfortable — this is very important to your control of the knife.

The right knife

Many knives are multipurpose, but common sense is required; for example, a short-bladed kitchen knife will never slice a loaf of bread neatly, and a bread knife isn't sharp enough to chop meat. So it's worth having a few different types in your kitchen.

The pot

When it comes to must-have, versatile pots, cast iron is 'The One'. Cast iron is rugged and durable (follow the manufacturer's care instructions to guarantee longevity); it's suitable for any heat source (except a microwave) and works best over medium or low heat, making it an economical purchase. For maximum versatility, choose a casserole dish with two integral cast-iron handles and a lid with a heat-resistant knob. The two handles make it easier to tip — when draining pasta, for example — and its heat-resistant material means you can start a dish off on the hob then transfer it to the oven. The downside is that cast iron is heavy — but it's worth its weight. It really is.

Holding heat
A cast-iron frying pan holds heat extremely well, so is perfect for cooking chicken pieces — the chicken browns beautifully and cooks through quickly without drying out.

Want more gizmos?

A good knife and pot are essential, but here is a small selection of really useful kitchen gadgetry to add to your basics. You'll find other suggestions throughout the book.

Gadget	Why do I need one?	Can I use an inexpensive model?
Handheld or 'stick' blender	Liquidizing soups and sauces; blending dips	A basic model does an adequate job; a high-speed model is a good investment later on
Fine mesh sieve	Rinsing grains; straining grains, pasta, veggies, stocks, sauces, yoghurt; sifting flour	A cheap plastic sieve is fine; a generously sized, very fine mesh metal sieve costs more but will get plenty of use and will last forever
Four-sided grater	Grating/slicing cheese and veggies; zesting citrus fruit	Cheap is fine
Coiled-wire whisk	Whipping eggs and light batters; making roux sauces; rescuing lumpy sauces; deglazing pans	Cheap is fine
Wooden spoons	Stirring, mixing and making you feel like a proper cook	Cheap is fine

FISH & SHELLFISH

Fish is popular worldwide and virtually all cultures have fish dishes in their culinary repertoire. Fish is incredibly quick to cook, is famed for its nutritional value and is endlessly versatile. It also tends to be expensive — so getting it right when it comes to buying and cooking is essential. This chapter tells you how.

Fresh with fish

Edible fish fall into one of two groups — 'white' or 'oily'. The difference? In white-fleshed fish, the oil is concentrated in the liver; in oily fish, the oil is distributed throughout, making the flesh firmer and darker. Simple as that!

1 Catch of the day

Fish are sold either whole or filleted. A really fresh whole fish is firm to the touch with a stiff tail and shiny, moist skin with scales intact. Look for clear, bright eyes and very red gills. Fillets should be firm and intact — avoid 'ragged' fillets that appear to be flaking. A very fresh white fish fillet is translucent, with no sign of discolouration. But the real giveaway? Fresh fish should have an appetizing smell of the sea — if it smells unpleasantly fishy, it's losing its charm.

2 Some like it raw

If you're planning to serve raw fish — for example, Japanese sushi or sashimi, Italian *pesce crudo* or carpaccio, French tartare, or Peruvian ceviche — it's absolutely essential to buy extremely fresh sushi-grade fish from a supplier you know and trust and use it immediately. If you can be hanging around at the harbour as the fishing boat docks, even better!

3 On ice

Fish is best eaten as soon as possible after purchase. A clever way to store it until you're ready to cook it is in a single layer on a plate or tray with crushed ice packed around it. You can freeze fish, but be aware that some 'fresh' fish has been previously frozen then defrosted for display and sale — check with the supplier and, if this is the case, do not refreeze.

Bed of ice
Use crushed ice rather than cubes for storing fish, so that the fish can nestle right into it.

4 Professional prep

A reliable fish supplier will prepare the fish for you, to whatever extent you wish (skin, bone, fillet), with skill and little waste. You really need a flexible filleting knife to skin or fillet a fish yourself — you can use your trusty cook's knife, but you're likely to sacrifice some of the flesh. To skin a fillet, place the fish skin-side down on a cutting board. Insert the knife between the skin and fillet and, holding the knife at an angle of about 25°, cut the fillet away from the skin with a sawing motion. Hold the liberated skin against the cutting board firmly as you cut.

5 Reasons to keep tinned tuna in your cupboard

1 Mix with hard-boiled eggs, olives, anchovies, tomatoes, lettuce, thin green beans and an oil-and-vinegar dressing for a salad niçoise.

2 Mix with soaked noodles and a creamy mushroom sauce and top with cheese or breadcrumbs for a comforting tuna bake.

3 Mix with pesto, soured cream and pasta and serve hot or cold.

4 Mix with tinned red kidney beans (rinsed and drained), sliced spring onions and celery, chopped herbs and a sharp, vinegary dressing for an instant dinner.

5 Mix with mashed potato, grated lemon zest, chopped parsley and capers; coat handfuls of the mixture with egg and breadcrumbs and fry for tuna fish cakes.

Sustainable fishing ID

Overfishing has become a major concern in the 21st century. This chart includes the traditional favourites; the suggested 'alternatives' help you identify a fish with the same type of flavour and texture, where possible, in case the one your recipe calls for is in the midst of a sustainability crisis.

Name	Type	Characteristics	How to cook	Alternatives
Cod	White, round	Flaky flesh, mild flavour	Pan-fry, poach, grill, roast, bake, steam	Haddock, hoki
Haddock	White, round	Flaky flesh, mild flavour	Pan-fry, poach, grill, roast, bake, steam	Cod, hoki
Hoki	White, round	Flaky flesh, mild flavour, few bones	Pan-fry, grill, bake	Cod, haddock
Tilapia	White, round	Flaky flesh, mild flavour	Pan-fry, grill, bake, barbecue (BBQ)	Farmed tilapia is a popular sustainable alternative to other white fish
Monkfish	White, round	Firm, meaty flesh, sweet flavour; only the tail is eaten	Pan-fry, grill, bake, BBQ	N/a
Red mullet	White, round	Firm flesh, rich flavour	Pan-fry, grill, bake, BBQ	Red snapper
Red snapper	White, round	Firm flesh, good flavour; usually cooked whole	Pan-fry, grill, bake, BBQ	Red mullet
Sea bass	White, round	Firm, moist flesh, sweet flavour; cooked whole or as fillets	Grill, bake, steam, BBQ	N/a
Brill	White, flat	Firm flesh, sweet flavour; cooked whole or as fillets	Pan-fry, grill, bake	Turbot, halibut
Halibut	White, flat	Meaty texture, excellent flavour	Pan-fry, grill, bake	Turbot, brill
Plaice	White, flat	Medium-soft flesh, distinctive flavour	Pan-fry, poach, grill	Sole, brill, dab
Dab	White, flat	Soft flesh, sweet flavour; cooked whole	Pan-fry, grill, bake	Sole, halibut, turbot
Sole (Dover/common)	White, flat	Firm but delicate flesh, subtle flavour — unusually, the flavour improves with keeping; cooked whole or as fillets	Pan-fry, poach, grill, roast, steam	Brill, lemon sole
Turbot	White, flat	Firm flesh, sweet flavour	Pan-fry, poach, grill, bake	Brill, halibut
Skate	White, flat	Moist, meaty flesh, good flavour; only the 'wings' are cooked	Poach, grill	N/a
Salmon (including Arctic char)	Oily	Firm pink flesh, good flavour; excellent smoked	Pan-fry, grill, bake, poach, steam, BBQ	Trout
Trout	Oily	Firm pink flesh, subtle flavour; cooked whole or as fillets	Pan-fry, grill, bake	Salmon
Tuna	Oily	Meaty flesh, distinctive flavour	Pan-fry, grill, bake, BBQ	N/a
Mackerel	Oily	Rich, meaty flesh, distinctive flavour; excellent smoked; cooked whole or as fillets	Pan-fry, poach, grill, bake, BBQ	N/a

The art of cooking fish

Fish lends itself to virtually every cooking method — but even the most robust fish is a delicate thing and needs to be treated with respect. Master the art, and the reward is culinary pleasure.

TRY IT

Batter with elegance A lighter alternative to a fish fillet fried in batter is to fry smaller pieces of fish in tempura batter. Experiment in a small way by whisking an egg yolk with 180 ml iced soda water, then stir ½ teaspoon cornflour into 100 grams (3½ oz) self-raising flour and add to the liquid. Stir until mixed but still lumpy, then simply drop slices of fish fillet into the batter to coat them, and deep-fry until delectably crisp and golden. Drain on kitchen paper and serve immediately.

6   Steak or fillet?

A fish 'steak' (above left) is cut perpendicular to the spine and is horseshoe-shaped with a wraparound skin and a roughly circular grain. A fish 'fillet' (above right) is cut parallel to the spine and is more evenly shaped, with the skin on the bottom, and the grain is chevron-like or diagonal. Essentially, there's no difference — but if you want pan-fried fish with a crisp skin, choose a fillet. It's much easier to control! Steaks lend themselves well to grilling, barbecuing and baking.

7   Melting flesh, crisp skin

A pan-fried fish fillet with crisp, golden-brown skin is a joy to behold (and to eat). This is how to achieve it.

1 Use a heavy-based frying pan and just enough unflavoured oil, such as rapeseed, to coat the pan evenly. Heat the frying pan over a medium-high heat and make sure it's very hot before you add the fish — the oil should be just smoking.

2 Dry the fish skin with kitchen paper. This is really important — you want the skin to sizzle when it hits the hot pan, not steam. Drying the skin also helps to prevent it sticking. Sprinkle the fillet on both sides with sea salt flakes.

3 Add the fish to the pan, skin-side down. Press the flesh lightly with a flexible fish spatula (or your fingers … if you dare) for a moment or two, until the fish settles with the skin flat on the frying pan.

4 When the skin is golden brown and gorgeous (lift the fillet with the spatula to peek), turn the fish gently and cook the other side.

Two sides are better than one
A crisp, golden-brown skin is a visual must, but the skinless side must look equally tempting.

8 Under the grill

As with pan-frying, a high temperature is important when grilling fish — start preheating the grill on its highest setting well in advance of cooking. Score whole round fish such as mackerel diagonally three times on each side. Brush the fish with melted butter before grilling and baste thick fillets and plump whole round fish with extra melted butter during cooking. Butter and fish — even oily fish — is a marriage made in heaven.

TRY IT

The fork test To check whether a chunky piece of fish is cooked all the way through, insert a fork into the thickest part, count to five, then rest the fork on your lower lip — the tines should feel warm.

Lock in the flavour
Lemon wedges are a classic garnish for fish, but try baking oily fish with thinly sliced citrus fruits for zingy flavour and as a foil for the richness.

9 How long?

The time it takes to pan-fry or grill fish depends on the thickness of the fish, the efficiency of the heat source and the temperature of the fish before cooking. Oily fish takes a little longer than lean white fish. As a rough guide, allow:
4–5 minutes on each side for a whole flat fish
5–6 minutes on each side for steaks and skinned fillets
7–8 minutes skin-side for fillets with skin; plus 3–4 minutes for the other side.

10 Is it done yet?

Overcooking fish is disastrous. To check for doneness, insert the tip of a sharp knife and separate the flesh slightly — it should be consistently opaque. If you're pan-frying, you can watch the flesh lose its raw, translucent look as the heat creeps up. The flesh will flake when it's cooked, look appetizingly moist and yield readily to the touch. When it's at this stage, serve immediately — the residual heat will continue to cook it. With experience, you'll know when to remove the fish from the heat just before it's perfectly cooked to allow for this.

TRY IT

On the bone Cooking a whole fish such as trout 'on the bone' has benefits — the bone holds the flesh together during cooking and reduces shrinkage; it conducts heat, which makes for more efficient cooking; and most importantly it enhances the flavour. The spine and bones come away from the cooked fish in one piece.

11 En papillote

Steamed fish is quick and easy to do in a steamer on the hob — just wrap the seasoned fillets in buttered aluminium foil, or even banana leaves if you can get your hands on them — but it's more fun to steam them *en papillote*, meaning 'in parchment'. It's a great way to steam tender fish fillets (not too thick — about 2.5 cm/1 inch) in the oven with julienned strips of vegetables and herbs. Here's how:

1 Cut a sheet of baking parchment into a heart shape large enough to hold the ingredients with a generous rim of unused paper surrounding them — it needs room to expand in the oven. Brush the baking parchment with melted butter.

2 Arrange the vegetables on one half of the parchment heart — just a few to avoid creating too much steam (French beans, purple sprouting broccoli and enoki mushrooms were used here). Place the fish fillet on top, then some herbs, strips of lemon zest and perhaps a few capers and sliced olives. Add a splash of liquid (wine is good, or olive oil) and season to taste.

3 Fold over the other half of the baking parchment heart and crimp the edges together tightly to form a seal.

4 The fun part! Transfer the package to a baking tray and place in a preheated oven (220°C/425°F) until the baking parchment magically expands and browns (about 10 minutes). Serve in the sealed package — the aromas released when you open it are divine.

12 Stuff it!

Roasting fish fillets or steaks is much like pan-frying — simply brush with olive oil or melted butter and place in a roasting pan in a hot oven (215°C/420°F), turning once. Roasting a whole individual fish is a great opportunity to add interest — try stuffing it with fresh herbs, a little crushed garlic and a slice or two of lemon (or orange or lime). Rinse the fish inside and out, then pat dry and score the skin diagonally on both sides before stuffing.

13 Saucy little number

You can bake fish very simply, in a little liquid — wine, cider, stock — but it really begs for a lovely sauce to wallow in while it's in the oven. A tomato-based sauce is always a winner. Place the fish in a buttered shallow ovenproof dish, cover with sauce, top with a layer of foil and bake at 190°C (375°F) for 20–25 minutes.

14 Court bouillon, sir?

Court bouillon is the posh name for poaching liquid. Combine equal quantities of water and a fruity, dry white wine with 'aromatics' — a *mirepoix* of carrot, onion and celery (see page 81), a bouquet garni (see page 98) and seasoning. The acidity of the wine coaxes the flavour from the other ingredients; lemon juice or white wine vinegar does the same job. Bring slowly to the boil, simmer for 30 minutes, then set aside for half an hour to cool and infuse (let go cold for cooking a whole fish).

15 Make peace with poaching

Poaching fish is a stress-free process — simply immerse the fish in liquid and simmer on a low heat for a few minutes. Done! The secret to successful poaching is to infuse the fish with flavour from the liquid, which you make in advance. After cooking, either strain the poaching liquid, discard the aromatics, add freshly cooked vegetables and serve with the fish fillet sitting in it, or use it to make a delicious sauce.

Less watered down
A fish kettle allows you to use the minimum quantity of water to immerse the fish, which concentrates the flavour of the aromatics in the poaching liquid.

TRY IT

Improvise! For poaching a large whole fish, such as salmon, improvise a fish kettle with a deep roasting pan (deep enough to allow the fish to be immersed in the water), a wire cooling rack to raise the fish above the heat source and an aluminium foil lid.

COURT BOUILLON FLAVOUR COMBOS

You can play around with the court bouillon concept to suit the fish you're cooking or to complement your tastes in cuisine. Here are a few ideas:

Milk + shallot + lemon zest
tarragon + flatfish

Rice wine vinegar + lemongrass + onion
garlic + fish sauce + salmon

Coconut milk + fish sauce + lime juice
garlic + chilli + cod

Vermouth + fennel + lemon zest

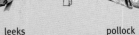

Italian bouquet garni + leeks + pollock

Mastering shellfish

Shellfish are strange creatures and can appear somewhat daunting to select, prepare and cook — but it's a simple matter of knowing what to look out for. Fortunately, shellfish are very obliging about providing clues to their freshness.

16   The two families

Shellfish come in two varieties: bivalves (aquatic mollusks with two hinged shells) and crustaceans (aquatic arthropods partially or completely protected by a hard external shell).

Bivalves

These include oysters, clams, mussels and scallops.

Selecting and storing: Buy from a reliable supplier (and if you're of a really nervous disposition, only buy commercially farmed and harvested bivalves). Make sure the bivalves look fresh — damp and shiny, with undamaged, tightly closed shells. Rinse, drain, place in a bowl (not plastic), cover tightly with a damp tea towel and refrigerate. Store oysters upright with the shell opening facing up. Eat on the day of purchase.

Preparing for the pot: Place uncooked bivalves in their shells in cold water and discard any that immediately float to the top. Scrape any barnacles off the survivors and scrub off the 'beards' with a stiff brush. Discard any with broken shells. Sharply tap any open specimens with a knife — if they remain open, discard those too. Rinse the rest thoroughly in cold water and drain well.

Crustaceans

These include lobsters, crabs and prawns.

Selecting and storing: Lobsters and crabs are best cooked live. Small lobsters (500 g–1.5 kg/1–3 pounds) are the most tender and coldwater lobsters are considered to be the best quality. Fresh crabs should feel heavy for their size. Prawns are available raw (but not live) or cooked. Cook live crustaceans as soon as possible after purchase to minimize trauma. If absolutely necessary, pack them in a cardboard box lined with a damp tea towel and store in the refrigerator. Cooked crustaceans keep in the refrigerator for up to three days.

Preparing for the pot: The challenge here is to avoid marauding claws — wear padded oven gloves (or gauntlets) to handle live lobsters and crabs. Placing them in the freezer for a few minutes before cooking dulls their senses.

TRY IT

Is there an 'R' in the month? An old (northern hemisphere) saying cautions us only to eat bivalve shellfish when there's an 'R' in the month — September to April. It's often assumed this is because they are poisonous during the summer months. There is potential for problems if the bivalves have been dining on toxic dinoflagellates, but licensed suppliers remove impurities through irradiation. However, the main reason is that bivalves throw all their energy into breeding during the summer months and simply aren't as yummy — so buy them in season.

TRY IT

Beef it up Oysters and beef make a happy partnership and beef in oyster sauce is a Chinese treasure of a dish. But take the time to make your own oyster sauce — commercial brands are likely to contain more artificial flavouring than actual oysters.

17 Secrets of a tender scallop

Scallops are sweet, succulent and need very little cooking — a moment too long and you're serving unpalatable rubber. The bright orange roes, or 'corals', cook in seconds.

1 First, dry the scallops thoroughly — place them on a plate lined with a folded (clean!) tea towel, put another tea towel on top and top with a plate and a weight.

2 Heat the frying pan over a medium-high heat until piping hot and add a drizzle of olive oil. The scallops should sizzle when they hit the pan.

3 Don't overcrowd the frying pan. If you're cooking lots of scallops, work in batches — overcrowding will lower the temperature.

4 Remember what order you placed the scallops in the pan, and turn them over in the same order. Scallops are ready when they turn opaque and pull apart easily.

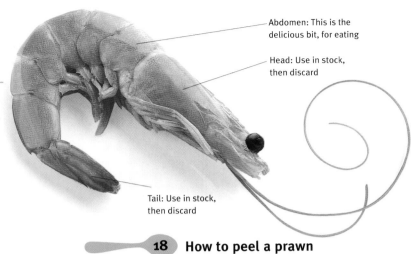

Abdomen: This is the delicious bit, for eating

Head: Use in stock, then discard

Tail: Use in stock, then discard

18 How to peel a prawn

Straighten out the prawn, holding the head in one hand and the tail in the other. Push the head and tail towards each other in a straight line, then pull apart again. The shell will slide off neatly.

Caramelized scallops
To achieve a good colour on scallops, add a pat of butter towards the end of the cooking time and baste the scallops. This doesn't mean you can get away with overcooking them, however!

TRY IT

Oyster knife The aim when shucking an oyster — the most highly prized shellfish — is to avoid damaging the precious flesh. An ergonomically designed oyster knife makes the job of oyster shucking easier. Even better is one that comes with a moulded cup to hold the oyster firmly in place. When using the knife, wrap your oyster-holding hand in a tea towel — use double thickness to be extra safe. Then it's all about finding the right place: hold the oyster curved-side down and look for a small gap at the pointy end of the shell. A twist of the knife and the shell should yield, releasing the flesh with minimum effort on your part.

Bouillabaisse — a taste of France

Virtually everywhere within sniffing distance of the sea
has its own version of a seafood soup. In France, it's
called 'bouillabaisse' and was originally cooked by
fishermen using rejects from the day's catch. You need
a combination of shellfish and white fish fillets (firm-
and soft-fleshed) — avoid oily fish. Remember to
allow time to marinate.

Ingredients
1.5 kg (3 lb) mixed seafood
150 g (5 oz) onions, chopped
1 large carrot, peeled and sliced
2 medium tomatoes, skinned and chopped
Crushed garlic cloves (as much as you can stand,
up to 2 tbsp)
Small sprig each of fennel, thyme and parsley
Small bay leaf
Strip of dried orange zest
120 ml olive oil
Pinch of powdered saffron
Salt and pepper
Fish stock (optional)

To serve:
Stale sourdough bread (see page 139)
Large handful of fresh flat-leaf parsley, chopped

1 Prepare the shellfish and cut the firm-fleshed fish fillets
into even-sized pieces.
2 Place the onions, carrot, tomatoes and garlic in a large
pan with the fennel, thyme, parsley, bay leaf and dried
orange zest. Add the prepared shellfish then the firm-
fleshed fish fillets. Drizzle with the olive oil, add the
saffron and season with salt and pepper. Cover and set
aside in a cool place for a few hours.
3 Add enough liquid (water or fish stock or a mixture)
to cover the fish, bring to a boil and boil rapidly for
7 minutes. Meanwhile, cut the soft-fleshed fish into
pieces. Add to the pan and boil for an additional
5–7 minutes. Check that the fish is cooked.
4 To serve, remove the fish and shellfish from the pan
and strain the stock into soup bowls lined with stale
sourdough bread. Sprinkle both fish and broth with
chopped flat-leaf parsley and serve separately, but at the
same time. Alternatively, serve the seafood, broth and
bread (not necessarily stale!) in a combination that
appeals to you.

FISH STOCK FLAVOUR COMBOS

Be creative and vary the herbs and spices in your fish stock. Stay with the basics — leek, celery, fennel bulb, parsley, bay leaf, wine — and experiment with the remaining flavourings.

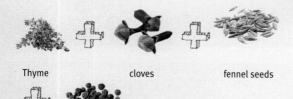

Thyme   cloves   fennel seeds

black peppercorns

Tarragon   dried orange zest   pink peppercorns

Lemon thyme   lovage   white peppercorns

Cardamom   lemongrass   lime zest

TRY IT

Dried orange zest Using a sharp knife, cut the ends off an unwaxed orange then score the peel into quarters and remove it. Pull away the bitter white pith (scrape off any that's left with the knife). Slice the zest into strips, spread them in a single layer on a baking tray lined with baking parchment and place in the oven set at its lowest temperature until dry and curled. Store in an airtight container in the refrigerator and use to add intrigue to whatever takes your fancy.

Shyness test
Live fresh mussels with open shells will close if you brush your hand over them.

19 Freshness test

Bivalves cooked in their shells, such as mussels and clams, should go into the cooking pot with their shells closed and emerge with their shells open. Discard any that remain closed. To tell if a live lobster is fresh, keep an eye on its tail as you cook it — it should curl neatly under the body. If this doesn't happen, discard the lobster.

20 Fabulous fish stock

A huge advantage of buying unprepared fish and shellfish is that you can transform all the discarded and rather unappetizing bits and pieces — bones, heads, skins, shells — into the most delicious fish stock. This makes a delectable base for soups, stews, seafood risotto and fish soufflé (reduce the stock for this). Use shellfish and white fish trimmings but not oily fish. Flavour the stock with leek, celery, fennel bulb, flat-leaf parsley, a dried bay leaf, a strip of lemon zest and a splash of white wine. Cover the ingredients with cold water, season to taste, then heat to simmering point and simmer gently for about 20 minutes. Pass the stock through a sieve lined with muslin.

Maximize your stock
For a quick fish soup, add steamed carrot slices, potato chunks and white fish fillet to your flavoursome stock.

Pork shoulder
with skin on

Pork shoulder

Pork belly

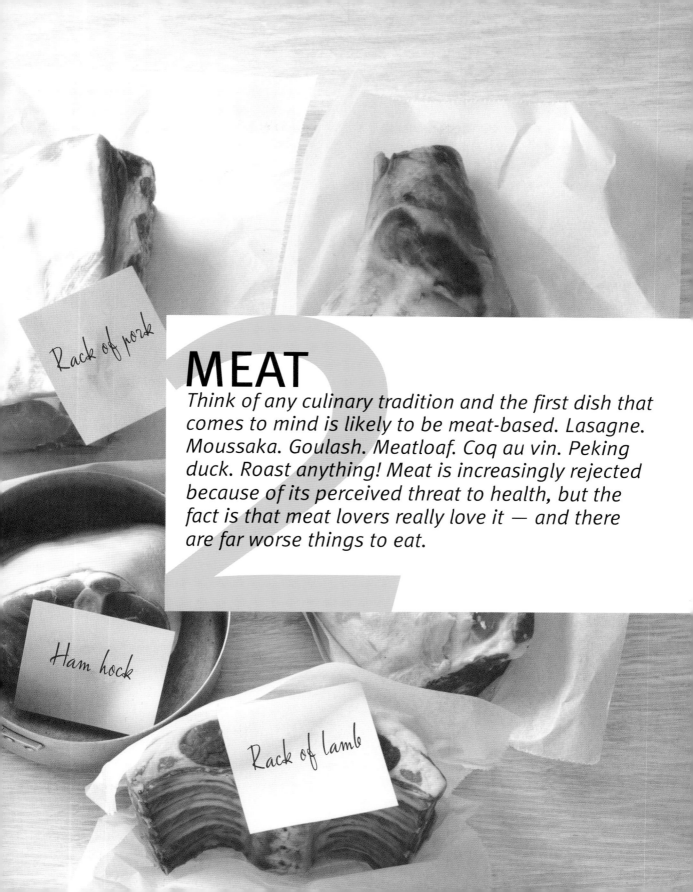

Rack of pork

MEAT

Think of any culinary tradition and the first dish that comes to mind is likely to be meat-based. Lasagne. Moussaka. Goulash. Meatloaf. Coq au vin. Peking duck. Roast anything! Meat is increasingly rejected because of its perceived threat to health, but the fact is that meat lovers really love it — and there are far worse things to eat.

Ham hock

Rack of lamb

Tenderizing meat

Even the most expensive meat can be tough and indigestible if it's not treated correctly, but there are plenty of ways to ensure a morsel that melts in your mouth, regardless of price and quality.

21 Understand the science

Cheaper cuts of meat tend to be high in connective tissue, which makes the meat tough — so breaking down the tissue is the key to a tender result. The secret of success is to cook the meat slowly at 70°C–80°C (160°F–180°F). At this temperature, the collagen that surrounds muscle fibres starts to break down into gelatin, coating the fibres and making the meat tender enough to cut with a fork. This works for any cooking technique, from braising to grilling on the barbecue.

Assorted steak cuts
Each cut of meat, in this case beef steak, has its own characteristics, be they centred on tenderness or flavour.

22 Know your cuts

Learning a little about the anatomy of the animal gives you an idea of where you can substitute one cut for another, or even one type of meat for another. Essentially, cuts from young animals or from the upper part of the animal are lower in connective tissue, whereas those from older animals or from the front or lower part — the areas where the muscles get most use — are higher in connective tissue. Remember these guidelines, familiarize yourself with dry/moist heat methods (see page 30) and get creative.

23 Choose your weapon

A manual meat tenderizer starts breaking down the connective tissue before cooking. Choose from the following:

Wooden Sometimes referred to as a 'meat mallet', this type has a spiky side and a smooth side. The spiky side breaks apart the muscle fibres and collagen bonds, softening the meat. The smooth side is used to flatten meat, particularly chicken breast, so that the meat cooks evenly. Remember to clean the tenderizer thoroughly after use, as wood can harbour bacteria.

Metal Similar to the wooden meat mallet, but made from aluminium or stainless steel. The weight of this type means it tenderizes with less effort than the lighter wooden mallet; on the other hand, it's more likely to flatten the meat, whether you want it flattened or not. Most metal mallets are dishwasher safe — a big advantage over the wooden one.

Rolling Less aggressive than a meat mallet, this type has razor-sharp blades that pierce the meat and cut through the tough fibres without flattening the meat.

TRY IT

Combining meat and dairy Milk, buttermilk and yoghurt contain lactic acid, which has a tenderizing effect on meat. Milk also keeps the flesh juicy as it cooks and enhances the flavour. The meat can be marinated — for example, a spicy, yoghurt-based tandoori marinade does wonders for chicken and lamb (see page 46). Alternatively, braise the meat gently in milk, as in the Italian dish *arrosto di maiale al latte* (pork in milk). The sauce is delicious and meant to be eaten with the meat — some curdling is inevitable, although whole milk and yoghurt are less likely to curdle than low-fat varieties.

24 Rest, rest and rest some more

When you pan-fry, grill, barbecue or roast meat, it's essential to let it rest before eating it to avoid a tough, dry exterior and a liquid interior that spills out unappetizingly when you cut into the meat. The muscle fibres contract with heat, especially on the surface of the meat where the temperature is highest. When the meat is rested, the temperature evens up as the outside cools and the centre continues cooking in the residual heat. The outer fibres relax and the moisture concentrated in the cooler centre of the meat is redistributed. How long you rest the meat depends on the size of the cut — a larger cut will, of course, need a longer resting time. If you have a meat thermometer (see page 31), check the temperature at the centre. When it's at 50°C (120°F), the meat's ready to eat.

Move to resting place
Resist the temptation to let meat rest in the roasting pan — the retained heat will carry on cooking the bottom of the meat, making it dry and tough.

25 Creating a flat surface

A preparation technique that cuts through meat horizontally, butterflying, leaves only one long side intact. This damages the fibres, helping to tenderize the meat, and the meat cooks faster and more evenly. It's also the technique to use to prepare a chop (see page 38) or chicken breast for stuffing. This technique works for a whole chicken by removing the backbone and flattening the bird. In this case, it's called 'spatchcocking'.

1 Cut down both sides of the backbone with poultry shears before removing the bone.

2 Turn the bird breast-side up and press down firmly in the centre of the breast, so that you hear the bones crunching.

Surely it's all just cooking?

It *is* all just cooking — but there are two basic ways to make the transition from raw to cooked meat, and the method you choose depends on the cut of meat.

26 Applying heat

It's essential to use the appropriate method for the cut of meat — it's possible both to ruin an expensive cut or to transform a cheap cut into a sublime one just thanks to the way it is cooked.

Dry heat Pan-searing, grilling, barbecuing and roasting are all methods of dry-heat cooking. Dry heat is suitable for cuts of meat that are lower in connective tissue and can cope with a high temperature and a short cooking time. It is possible to get a tender result with a cheaper cut as long as you sear the meat at the higher temperature, then reduce the temperature and cook the meat slowly to break down the connective tissue (see page 28).

Moist heat This involves some form of liquid, ideally something such as wine or cider that contributes to breaking down the connective tissue as this is the method to use for cheaper, tougher cuts. Examples of moist heat cooking are braising and stewing. With braising, the meat is first seared, then partially covered in liquid and simmered slowly. With stewing, the meat is again seared first, then immersed completely in liquid. In both cases, the meat is cooked at the optimum temperature for breaking down the connective tissue.

Preheated coals
Make sure the coals are really hot before you cook meat on a barbecue. When they're a uniform grey, you're good to go.

All under control
Tying an unwieldy cut of meat neatly with string makes it easier to brown, cook and carve.

27 Successful browning

When browning meat, it's necessary to observe a few rules. The object of the exercise is to sear the outside of the meat and seal in the moisture, so the end result is tender, succulent and flavourful, with a caramelized crust.

1 Dry the meat thoroughly with kitchen paper. If you skip this step, the meat will steam rather than brown. If you're cutting the meat into cubes for your recipe, dry the cubes.
2 Heat the frying pan over a medium-high heat. It must be hot enough to sear the outside of the meat immediately.
3 Add a little oil to the frying pan — just enough to prevent the meat from sticking.
4 As soon as one surface is seared to a rich, dark brown, turn the meat to sear the next. If you have lots of small pieces, a pair of tongs is an efficient tool for turning rapidly.

If you're browning a lot of meat, work in batches so you can keep up with turning it. The same applies if your frying pan is too small for the quantity of meat — work in batches so each piece of meat has plenty of space.

28 Raising the temperature

A cut of meat will struggle to roast evenly straight from the refrigerator, so bring it to room temperature before committing it to the oven. Remove the wrapping and cover it with a clean tea towel to absorb any moisture from the surface.

29 Calculating roasting times

If you've invested in an expensive cut of meat to roast, you want to get it right. You can calculate the time needed according to the weight of the meat (see below), but the more reliable (and, if your oven is unreliable, more reassuring) method is to use a thermometer. Remember that the meat will continue to cook in the residual heat once it's out of the oven, so remove it when the internal temperature is about 5°C (40°F) below the ideal for the result you want. As a rough guide to oven temperature, start off at 220°C (425°F) for 20–30 minutes, then reduce to 180°C (350°F) for the remainder of the cooking time.

TRY IT

Going pro *Sous vide* — 'under pressure' — is a cooking method beloved of professional chefs. The idea is to vacuum-pack the meat (or other food item) and immerse it in a tank of hot water maintained at a precise temperature, requiring far more hours of cooking time than a more traditional method, but with amazing results. For this type of cooking, you need an efficient vacuum-sealer and a tank.

Meat	Best cut	Minutes per 450 g (per pound)	Recommended minimum safe internal temperature
Beef	Sirloin or double rib, on the bone	15 (rare) + 15 extra minutes (medium) + 30 extra minutes (well done)	62°C (145°F)
Pork	Leg or loin	35	62°C (145°F)
Lamb	Leg or shoulder	20 (rare) + 10 extra minutes (medium) + 15–20 extra minutes (well done)	62°C (145°F)
Chicken	Whole	20 + 10–20 extra minutes	74°C (165°F)

TRY IT

The skewer test One effective method of checking whether roasted beef or lamb is cooked is to insert a skewer into the thickest part. If it's cool when you take it out, the meat is rare; if it's warm, the meat is medium; if it's hot, the meat is well done.

30 Meat thermometer

A meat thermometer is a great confidence booster — it tells you when your meat is cooked to a 'safe-to-eat' temperature and to perfection for your preference.

Instant-read This type is all-purpose and the one to use for casseroles, etc., as you insert it at intervals. Despite its encouraging name, it's usually relatively slow to register an accurate reading of the current temperature.

Ovenproof This one is ideal for roasts — insert it into the meat at the start of cooking and leave it there so it constantly registers an accurate current reading. The most sophisticated version beeps to alert you when your meat has reached the optimum temperature for the type of meat and desired level of doneness. Always insert the thermometer into the thickest part of the meat but away from any bone.

Protect your hands
Ovenproof meat thermometers get hot, so remember to wear an oven glove when removing one.

Beef: The ultimate red meat

Beef stands in solitary magnificence as a steak or roast and mingles happily with a multitude of other ingredients in much-loved dishes such as lasagne.

Good breeding
The method by which beef cattle are raised is more important than the breed, but if you're keen to know what breed you're buying, a good butcher will know the provenance.

31 A fanfare for quality

With high levels of saturated fat, beef has become less popular than low-fat options. Health issues — and those concerning animal welfare — aside, it's worth cutting down on frequent meat consumption in order to splurge on an occasional top-quality cut. The very best beef is raised organically and grass-fed right up until slaughter — and it's not just about the flavour, although this is undeniably superior. Beef produced in this way is richest in essential fatty acids (EFAs), especially omega-3, and lowest in saturated fat. Great news for the health-conscious cook! Some beef cattle are raised on grass but 'finished' on cereals, immediately reducing the levels of EFAs and raising the saturated fats — so make sure you know exactly what you're paying for.

32 Veal-ly tasty

Most beef is raised specifically for the purpose, but veal makes practical use of male calves born to dairy cattle, which would otherwise be slaughtered at birth. High-welfare rose veal is a delicately flavoured pink meat that works well in all the traditional veal recipes such as Wiener schnitzel, osso buco and *saltimbocca*.

Ideal for beginners
Rose veal has a mild beef flavour, and because it's young, it's always tender — reassuring for a novice cook.

33 Aged meat

Hanging meat — the whole or halved carcass is hung, rather than individual cuts — in a controlled environment after slaughter both tenderizes it and concentrates the flavour. Lamb, pork and poultry are best aged for a week, whereas beef should hang for a minimum of 21 days. If you take your meat eating seriously, or for special occasions, seek out a specialist supplier to provide you with aged meat.

34 Fat and flavour

Fat makes a major contribution to the undeniable umami of meat, especially beef. So if it's natural flavour you're after, look for a cut with a good marbling of fat. Fat also helps with tenderness in a cheaper cut, because it melts as it warms with cooking, lubricating the muscle fibres.

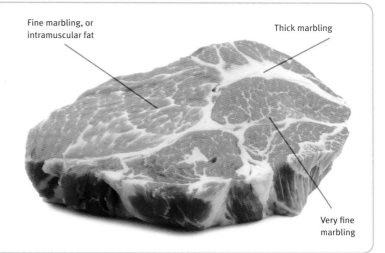

Fine marbling, or intramuscular fat

Thick marbling

Very fine marbling

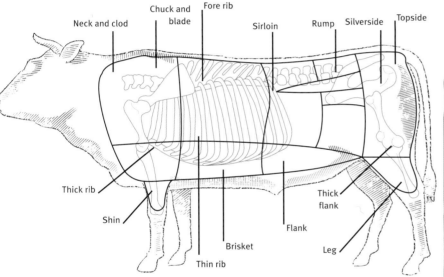

Neck and clod

Chuck and blade

Fore rib

Sirloin

Rump

Silverside

Topside

Thick rib

Shin

Thin rib

Brisket

Flank

Thick flank

Leg

Customize it

If you make it yourself, you can make it your own — experiment with combinations of onion, garlic, spices and herbs until you find your magic blend.

35 Key cuts

Butchery is a skill best left to the experts, but familiarity with the terminology enables you to identify the best cut for the type of dish you're cooking.

Dry heat The prime cuts for roasting are taken from the middle and hindquarters of the animal: silverside, rump and sirloin, for example. Top-side and chuck cuts are also worth considering. For pan-frying or grilling, choose a tender cut, ideally with fine streaks of fat for flavour: fillet steak, porterhouse, T-bone, sirloin, skirt.

Moist heat This is where the tough, less expensive cuts come into their own — not because you can get away with a cheap compromise, but because they actually produce a better result. Go for brisket or chuck for pot roasting, chuck or silverside for stews.

TRY IT

DIY mince It only takes minutes to prepare your own minced beef for burgers, meatloaf or meat sauce. Cheap cuts are fine for this as the chopping action breaks down the connective tissue. Slice the beef evenly, then cut it into dice. Grip the handles of two cook's knives in one hand, anchoring the knife tips on the cutting board with the other hand. Chop rapidly back and forth across the meat until minced.

36 Comforting pot roast

Pot roasting is a great way to cook a cheap cut of beef, such as brisket or chuck. It's less labour-intensive than dry heat roasting — you simply sear the meat on all sides, partially cover it in liquid (to come halfway up the meat) and place it in an oven at low heat (150°C/300°F) for about 4 hours. The technique is essentially braising, but you still end up with a lovely joint of meat, with a caramelized crust, that you can carve. You'll need a heavy casserole dish with a tight-fitting lid – if your piece of meat is too large to fit comfortably on the base, roll it (fat-side out) and secure it three or four times along its length with kitchen twine. For a really good flavour, cook the meat in well-seasoned beef stock or red wine, with onions, carrots and a bouquet garni.

Natural thickeners
Always add root vegetables, such as the carrots shown here, to a braised dish – the veggies will release starch and thicken the liquid.

37 Fingertip test for steak

Experienced chefs can tell when a steak has reached the desired level of doneness just by pressing the cooked meat with a fingertip. The more the meat is cooked, the less springy it becomes. To familiarize yourself with how a cooked steak should feel, practise the fingertip test on the fleshy part of your palm at the base of the thumb. Position your thumb and fingers as shown in the pictures and use the fingertip of your free hand to press down where indicated.

Raw: Feels very soft.

Rare: Feels soft and bouncy.

Medium: Some give; feels springy.

Well done: No give; feels firm.

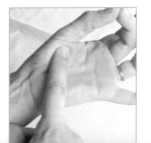
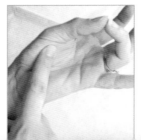

38   Mighty meaty

A good beef stock begins with marrow bones and the holy trinity (see page 81) of onion, carrot and celery. If you can use marrow bones from a grass-fed beast, so much the better.

Ingredients
900 g (2 lb) bones
2 onions, peeled and quartered
2 carrots, peeled and roughly chopped
3 sticks of celery, roughly chopped
1 bay leaf
8 peppercorns
3 fresh flat-leaf parsley stalks
Sprig of fresh thyme

1 Place all the ingredients in a saucepan and cover with cold water.
2 Bring to the boil and skim off and discard the scum.
3 Cover and simmer very gently for 3–4 hours, skimming off any more scum.
4 Strain the stock into a large bowl (see below), allow it to cool, then chill in the refrigerator overnight.
5 Skim the fat off the surface.

Intensify flavour
For an even more intense beef stock, first roast the beef bones for about 45 minutes, then add them to the vegetables, along with the roasting juices.

Smooth end result
Pass the finished stock through the finest sieve you have.

FIX IT

Too tough? Salvage a disappointingly tough steak or pot roast by cooking it some more, in plenty of liquid. Add enough to cover the meat — ideally beef broth and wine in equal quantities, but even water will do. Bring the liquid to a boil, then reduce to a simmer, cover tightly and cook slowly — around 20 minutes for a steak and 2–6 hours for a pot roast.

Versatile pork

Pork is a meat with plenty of potential. It roasts and braises beautifully, makes juicy, flavourful sausages and of course provides bacon, which enhances so many other ingredients.

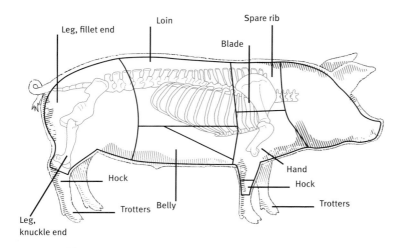

Leg, fillet end
Loin
Spare rib
Blade
Leg, knuckle end
Hock
Trotters
Belly
Hand
Hock
Trotters

39 Pan-fried chops

For pan-frying, choose a generous 2.5 cm- (1 inch-) thick chop, with the fat on. Make diagonal slashes in the fat to prevent the chop buckling as it cooks. Heat the frying pan with no additional fat and, using tongs, lower the chop in fat-side down. Hold it with the tongs until the fat browns and crisps. You can then cook the chop in the fat released into the frying pan.

Drain away
If your pan-fried chop seems greasy when it comes out of the pan, drain it on crumpled baking parchment.

40 How to identify top-quality pork

Pigs are natural foragers and left to their own devices would roam around and produce tender, flavourful, fairly red meat with a good balance of fat. Farmed pork, fattened rapidly on cereals, tends to be pale and damp in appearance and bland in flavour, whereas good-quality free-range organic pork has firm, pink flesh with no trace of excess moisture.

41 Key cuts

Pork is a meat that is sold fresh for cooking in dry or moist heat but, of all the meats, is also the one traditionally preserved by smoking or curing. Preserved products range from spiced air-dried sausages, such as salami and chorizo, to bacon and hams, including prosciutto, pancetta and the exceptionally fine Spanish *jamón ibérico*.

Dry heat The best cuts for roasting are belly, spare rib, shoulder, hand, boned blade and loin, especially the tenderloin. The tenderloin is also good for pan-frying or grilling, as are spare rib or loin chops.
Moist heat Spare rib and shoulder work well in braises and stews.

42 Not just a weekend treat

Roast pork with crisp crackling is something special to look forward to at the weekend. However, pork and pork products are a versatile option for midweek — and if you're too tired to cook, a slice or two of good ham with a salad and sourdough bread is a perfect dinner.

44 The crispest crackling

Aficionados would willingly sacrifice all other forms of fat for a week (or longer) for a serving of roast pork rack with crisp crackling. Choose a cut with a thick, even layer of fat beneath the skin.

1 The skin must be very dry to crisp up properly, so take the pork out of the refrigerator a half hour before cooking and remove the wrapping.

2 Score the skin evenly in a 2.5 cm (1-inch) diagonal criss-cross pattern with the tip of a sharp knife, but avoid cutting into the flesh.

3 Massage the skin generously with fine sea salt, blot thoroughly with kitchen paper and set aside to dry. Meanwhile, preheat the oven to 240°C (475°F).

4 Blot the skin again if it looks at all damp. Roast the pork (skin-side up — not necessarily an obvious point!) for 20 minutes, then reduce the heat to 180°C (350°F) for the remainder of the cooking time.

43 Naughty but nice

You can roast crackling separately. Score the skin before slicing it off the meat in one piece with some of the fat layer. Blot it with kitchen paper, brush lightly with olive oil and massage with salt. Place on a shallow roasting pan and roast at 220°C (425°F) for 15–20 minutes, or until crisp and golden.

45

A marriage made in heaven

Pork, apples and sage are a happy partnership — the sharp/sweet apples and earthy sage balancing the richness of the meat. If you can source organic pork that's been raised in an orchard, grazing on fallen apples, you're off to a great start. Otherwise, cook the pork in cider or with apple slices and sage, or fill a chop or loin with apple and sage stuffing. Pork is also good served with apple sauce or caramelized apple slices and a crisp sage garnish, or a cider or Calvados and sage sauce.

1

4

46 **Stuffed chop**

A stuffed pork chop is a quick and easy way to satisfy a midweek roast pork craving (and you can practise your 'butterflying' technique). If you buy chops with the skin on, you can even make separate crackling strips (see page 37).

Ingredients

4 thick boneless pork chops
2 tsp olive oil
1 large echalion (banana) shallot, finely chopped
80 g (3 oz) fresh white breadcrumbs
1 small eating apple, finely chopped
1 tbsp fresh sage leaves, finely chopped
1 tsp finely grated lemon zest
1 small egg, beaten
Salt and pepper, to taste

1 Butterfly the pork chops (see page 29), leaving a 1 cm (½-inch) join.
2 Heat the oil in a small pan over a medium heat and gently sauté the shallot until soft but not coloured.
3 Stir the shallot into the breadcrumbs with the remaining ingredients and season to taste with salt and pepper.
4 Divide the stuffing among the pork chops and skewer the opening with cocktail sticks to prevent the stuffing from escaping. Brush the chops lightly with oil on both sides.
5 Brown in an ovenproof frying pan for 1 minute on each side, then transfer to a preheated oven (200°C/400°F) and roast for 10–15 minutes, until cooked through.

Perfectly smoked
If you're oven-cooking pulled pork, mix a little smoked paprika with salt and dark brown sugar and massage it into the meat for that smoky barbecue flavour.

47 The ultimate test

Pulled pork is the most effective proof of tenderness in meat — so tender it can be pulled apart with nothing more than two forks, or even your fingers. The cut of choice is the upper part of the shoulder, known in the US as the Boston butt, with the bone in. The best pulled pork is cooked very, very slowly on a barbecue to break down the connective tissue. However, it's possible to create a passable imitation in terms of tenderness, albeit without the authentic smokiness, in the oven.

1 Brown the pork for 40 minutes in a preheated hot oven (220°C/425°F).
2 Reduce the temperature to 120°C (250°F), cover the roasting pan completely with a tight-fitting foil lid and cook for a further 6 hours, or until the meat is meltingly tender.
3 Increase the heat to 220°C (425°F) and cook, uncovered, for an additional 10 minutes. Remember to let it rest!

48 Reasons to keep some pancetta in your fridge

1 Sauté chopped pancetta before adding vegetables to the pan for a soup — the flavour will infuse the vegetables and give the whole thing a lift. Especially good with lentils.

2 Grill pancetta until crisp then crumble over a salad. It's delicious with peppery watercress, astringent rocket or iron-rich spinach and sweet fruits such as pear, peach or fig.

3 Use sautéed pancetta lardons in egg dishes such as omelettes, frittatas or quiches.

4 Sauté strips of pancetta in a frying pan, add lightly steamed vegetables such as cabbage, Brussels sprouts, broad beans and peas, and toss to combine.

5 Wrap thin slices of pancetta around meat, poultry, fish fillets or vegetables. It works really well with the most unlikely things, such as beef and salmon.

It's a wrap
A slice of pancetta is useful for anchoring herbs or thin strips of vegetable, such as courgette, to a fish fillet.

Create your own sizzle

Sausage-making is an art worth acquiring. Apart from the fact that you'll know exactly what went into your sausage (always an advantage), there's endless fun to be had enhancing the flavour with herbs, spices, a splash of wine ...

49　Artisan sausages

Sausages come in many forms, often with the intention of preserving the meat. This recipe is for a fresh pork sausage, to be eaten immediately — for breakfast, with colcannon (see page 84), in a casserole. Your favourite way!

Ingredients
Makes 8

450 g (1 lb) pork
3–5 tbsp dried breadcrumbs
(homemade from good white bread)
Flavourings (see flavour combo panel for ideas), prepared as necessary
3–5 tbsp cold water
Sea salt, to taste
Casing

1 Decide on the texture you want for your sausages and mince the meat accordingly. If you don't have a mincer, see page 33 for the technique for mincing meat with knives.
2 Add the dried breadcrumbs, together with the flavourings and salt, and mix thoroughly with your hands.
3 Add the water (use the same volume as breadcrumbs) and mix again. If you overdo the water, the sausages will explode when you cook them.
4 Open up one end of the casing and place it over the funnel or stuffing tube attachment (see the sausage stuffer, page 41).

5 Feed the mixture into the casing. Tie off one end of the casing to thwart escape, then twist the casing a few times at regular intervals to form the individual sausage links.

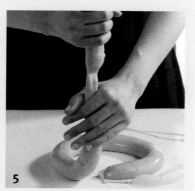

TRY IT

Think ahead! Cube the meat, season with salt and freeze for 30 minutes before mincing. This makes it easier to mince.

50　The casing

The best casing for sausages is a long length of all-natural animal intestine (hog or sheep), available from specialist suppliers. If the thought of that sends you into a fit of squeamishness, take heart — the intestines are thoroughly cleaned and look perfectly inoffensive. They're preserved in salt so they need to be soaked in water for a minimum of 2 hours before use. Hog casings are more robust than sheep.

The 'yum' factor
Try wrapping the sausages in a strip of pancetta or thinly sliced bacon before frying.

51 Making great sausages

Golden rules

1 Use good-quality meat — half should be a lean cut, such as back (loin), and half a cut streaked with plenty of fat, such as shoulder (blade), to make a moist, flavourful sausage.

2 Fry a spoonful of the meat mixture before filling the casing to check you're happy with the seasoning. It's your last chance to make adjustments.

3 Fill the casing so it's neither bursting to capacity nor full of air pockets. Either extreme will give a less than perfect result when it comes to cooking the sausage.

52 How to cook a succulent sausage

Sausages benefit from long, slow cooking rather than high-temperature frying, and they need you to be in attendance for half an hour or so. Do not prick the skin — the fat in the meat contributes much to the deliciousness and succulence of the sausage, so you want it kept in the skin, not seeping out through little perforations. Warm the frying pan over a fairly low heat and oil it lightly. Brush each sausage generously with oil before adding to the frying pan. Cook gently, rolling the sausages constantly, until the skins are evenly caramelized — by which time the sausages will be cooked through.

SAUSAGE FLAVOUR COMBOS

You can create a completely different sausage mood simply by changing the flavourings. Here are a few ideas:

Sage   nutmeg   white pepper

Red wine   garlic   rosemary

thyme

Pimentón   garlic   fennel seeds

black pepper

53 The sausage stuffer — can you live without it?

The most economical method of uniting the meat mixture with the casing is to hand-fill the casing via a funnel (available from specialist suppliers). Easier and more efficient by far is a manual grinder with a stuffing tube attachment (still relatively inexpensive, and both grinds and fills) or a manual stuffer (quite expensive, and you need some means of grinding). Beyond that, the equipment is power-driven and can be really expensive. So whether you can live without a sausage stuffer depends on how seriously you intend to take your sausage-making.

Lively lamb

Lamb stands up well to gutsy flavours such as garlic, spices and pungent herbs, so it fits comfortably in the culinary traditions of many cultures around the globe.

 54 How old is that lamb?

Lamb in its first year has pale to dark pink meat, depending on its age, and is at its most tender, with a delicate flavour. Past a year, the meat is darker and the flavour richer, but it's less tender. Past two years, the flavour is really well developed but the flesh is tougher and needs some method of tenderizing. If possible, choose organic grass-fed spring lamb (under a year old) that's been hung for a week.

TRY IT

Salt-marsh lamb If you can track it down, salt-marsh lamb takes the lamb-eating experience to a whole new level. In France, it's known as *pre-salé* ('pre-salted') and is so revered that lamb from Baie de Somme carries an AOC distinction (Appellation d'Origine Contrôlée). Salt-marsh lamb takes on the flavour of the rich diversity of coastal pasture on which it's grazed. Enhance the lamb even more by serving it with samphire (see page 85).

 55 Orange mint sauce

Mint sauce is a delicious accompaniment to roast lamb. The classic recipe is finely chopped fresh mint leaves steeped in boiling water with a pinch of sea salt and 1 tablespoon caster sugar. When the water cools, stir in 4 tablespoons of white wine vinegar. But lamb marries well with orange, so try using orange mint (with 1 teaspoon of sugar) and replace 1 tablespoon of the white wine vinegar with orange balsamic vinegar.

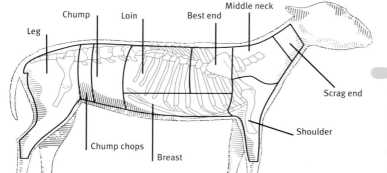

 56 Roast with lavender

An unusual take on traditional roast lamb with rosemary is to replace the rosemary with fragrant lavender flowers. There are several ways to do this:

Sprigs Make slits in the lamb with the tip of a sharp knife and insert sprigs of fresh lavender.

Rub Massage olive oil into the lamb, then rub in fresh or culinary lavender 'heads' (the tiny individual buds).

Seasoning Grind sea salt flakes with fresh or culinary lavender heads, using a pestle and mortar, and sprinkle generously over the lamb.

Honey Massage olive oil into the lamb, followed by lavender honey.

Added zing
Add grated lemon zest to a herb crust to complement the sweetness of the lamb.

57 Key cuts

Because lamb is young and still tender, most cuts lend themselves readily to roasting, but the best are breast, shoulder, front rib, loin and leg. Steaks and chops made from the loin and leg are good for pan-frying or grilling. The shanks and shoulder are excellent for slow-cooking.

Eastern influence: Kofte

Lamb is widely used in Middle Eastern cooking and kofte — minced lamb kebabs — are subtly spicy and irresistible. You can mince the lamb at home if you wish, using the technique on page 33. Shoulder of lamb, streaked with fat, is the perfect cut for this. Kofte are best made well in advance to allow the flavours to develop.

Ingredients
450 g (1 lb) minced lamb
1 small onion
1 tsp ground cumin
1 tsp ground coriander
$\frac{1}{4}$ tsp garam masala
$\frac{1}{4}$ tsp cayenne pepper
2 tbsp fresh coriander or flat-leaf parsley, very finely chopped
2 tbsp plain yoghurt
Sea salt, to taste

To serve:
Flatbreads such as pitta
Strained yoghurt
Salad leaves

1 Place the minced lamb in a large bowl.
2 Grate the onion very finely into a separate bowl, then transfer it to a fine sieve and squeeze out as much of the liquid as possible. Add the onion to the lamb, discarding the liquid.
3 Add the remaining ingredients and combine the mixture with your hands.
4 Form into balls or cigar shapes and chill in the refrigerator for up to 12 hours.
5 Cook in a lightly oiled frying pan over a medium heat, in batches if necessary, until golden brown all over. Alternatively, cook on a griddle pan (oil the kofte rather than the griddle), or under the grill. Serve with flatbreads, yoghurt and salad leaves.

Popular poultry

Chicken is without a doubt the most popular poultry, being quick to cook and endlessly versatile, and because of its perceived health benefits in terms of fat content. Turkey is, of course, the bird of choice for a grand occasion. Duck and goose also fall under the poultry umbrella.

Practical nostalgia
A vintage-style enamel roaster costs next to nothing and, best of all, has a self-basting lid.

 **58 Succulent roast**

One of the great joys of a roast chicken is returning to the carcass to pick off the bits that were missed in the carving. Make sure there's moist meat and plenty of flavour to look forward to! A simple trick is to prick a small unwaxed lemon and place it in the cavity of the bird, along with a few sprigs of fresh rosemary or thyme. That takes care of the flavour from the inside out. For the outside in, mash crushed garlic, finely grated lemon zest and fresh rosemary or thyme leaves into softened unsalted butter. Carefully loosen the skin over the breast of the chicken, leaving one end intact, and slather the herbed butter over the flesh (under the skin).

59 Is free-range worth it?

A free-range chicken eats its natural diet of whatever it finds in pasture — grass, herbs, clover, wild seeds and insects — which results in sweeter, tastier and more nutritious flesh than a chicken raised on a grain-based diet designed only to promote rapid growth. A free-range chicken also has room to flap its wings, which exercises the breast muscles, providing firmer, meatier flesh. It will cost considerably more so it's up to you to balance the benefits with your budget.

Golden rules

Roast chicken

1 Allow the chicken to come to room temperature before cooking. This is especially important with poultry as you run the risk of the breast cooking quickly and drying out while the thick leg meat is still struggling to warm up.

2 Dry the chicken thoroughly with kitchen paper.

3 Cook the chicken at 190°C (375°F) until 10 minutes before the end of the calculated roasting time (see page 31), then increase the heat to 220°C (425°F) to crisp the skin.

TRY IT

Rich stock To make a richer, darker chicken stock, chop chicken wings into pieces and caramelize them in a little bland oil, such as rapeseed, in a hot oven (230°C/450°F). Remove the chicken wings, deglaze the roasting pan and place the chicken wings and juices in a pan to complete the recipe.

61 Stocking up

If you don't want to use your stock immediately, let it cool, pour it into a jar with a tight-fitting lid or a freezer-proof container, and store it in the refrigerator for up to three days or the freezer for up to three months.

Light and elegant stock

A homemade chicken stock is one of the most useful items in your culinary repertoire. Besides adding depth to any chicken dish, it also adds flavour to soup, sauces, any type of risotto, grains such as couscous and quinoa — anything that needs a little taste boost. It's a great way to make use of a whole chicken — after jointing or cooking, the carcass is left to enhance your stock.

Ingredients
1 cooked chicken carcass, broken up
1 onion, peeled and quartered
1 carrot, peeled and roughly chopped
1 stick of celery, roughly chopped
1 leek, roughly chopped
$\frac{1}{4}$ small fennel bulb, roughly chopped (optional)
6 peppercorns
3 fresh flat-leaf parsley stalks
Sprig of fresh thyme

1 Place all the ingredients in a pan and cover with cold water. Bring to the boil and skim off and discard the scum.
2 Cover and simmer very gently for 2 hours, skimming off any more scum.
3 Strain the stock into a large bowl, let it cool, then chill in the refrigerator overnight. Skim any fat off the surface.

62 Tandoori chicken marinade

In India, this delectable spiced meat is cooked in a special tandoor oven over a charcoal or wood fire, but it works well on a barbecue. Add a little red food colouring to the marinade to achieve the traditional bright red colour, or leave it au naturel.

Ingredients

1 small onion, chopped
1 garlic clove
Knob of fresh root ginger
1 or 2 hot green chillies, to taste

450 ml yoghurt
2 tsp garam masala (see page 103)
Red food colouring (optional)

1 Assemble the ingredients.

2 Mix the ingredients using a hand- or stick-blender until very smooth.

3 Pour the marinade over the chicken pieces. Remember to turn the chicken occasionally to make sure it's well coated.

Charred to perfection
The authentic way to serve tandoori chicken is with naan bread, which traditionally is also cooked in the tandoor, giving it those yummy charred bits.

Reasons 63 to keep some chicken breasts in your freezer

(Defrost your chicken thoroughly and according to food-safety guidelines before attempting any of the following.)

1 Always available for making chicken soup for the soul. Everyone needs it sometime or other!

2 Slice it thinly for a simple stir-fry — there's every reason to cook a proper meal, even in the middle of the week.

3 Butterfly it, stuff it with ham and cheese, coat it in egg and breadcrumbs and bake it for a 1970s revival dish — chicken cordon bleu.

4 Add chunks to a mushroom and tarragon béchamel sauce and top with puff pastry for a quick pie.

5 Wrap in prosciutto, skewer a sage leaf on top and pan-fry. Serve in slices on a mushroom risotto.

TRY IT

Good 'smoking' teas The tea you use influences the flavour of the smoke. Try teas with very distinctive flavours such as jasmine, Earl Grey, gunpowder, keemun, rooibos, lapsang souchong or cardamom.

Smokin'!

Smoked meat takes on the essence of whatever it's smoked over and loose tea leaves (or the contents of tea bags) work particularly well. Create your own indoor smoker for chicken or duck breasts using a wok or, for real homemade charm, an old biscuit tin, with a rack and a tight-fitting lid.

1 Line the base of the wok or tin with aluminium foil.
2 Mix together 75 g (2½ oz) raw long-grain rice, 50 g (2 oz) brown sugar and 25 g (1 oz) loose tea leaves and sprinkle the mixture over the foil. Place the rack on top.
3 Place the wok or tin over a high heat until the tea mixture starts to smoke, then place the chicken or duck breasts on the rack and put on the lid.
4 Reduce the heat to medium-low for about 15 minutes, until the meat is cooked through. Two things to remember: be prepared for things to get a bit smoky and hot — if you're using a biscuit tin, wear oven gloves to pick it up.

64 Once it's smoked

Smoked chicken or duck is delicious with salad leaves — throw in a few orange slices with the chicken, and fresh figs or dried cherries with the duck, and use a basic vinaigrette dressing. Or try shredding the meat and adding it to a simple stir-fry.

Pretty tasty
Shred smoked chicken into a salad of hot, peppery watercress and sweet tomatoes.

GRAINS & LEGUMES

*Grains and legumes are cupboard treasures —
they have a generous shelf life, are not too
difficult to prepare and lend themselves to
endless recipe possibilities. From beans and
lentils to rice, pasta and a few more unusual
grains from around the world, this chapter
reveals the secrets of these must-have
ingredients.*

Rice is nice

Some varieties of rice cook quickly and the grains are light and fluffy; others take longer and the grains remain chewy and satisfying; and some need tender loving care to produce the desired result.

 65 Why doesn't mine come out like that?

White long-grain rice is something that, if you get it wrong once, you start to fear. The benchmark of perfection is when the cooked grains remain separate. To achieve this, rinse the rice under cold running water, then soak it in cold water for 30 minutes. This softens the rice and stops it from splitting during cooking — and no splitting means no sticking. Drain the rice after soaking and cook it in fresh water.

TRY IT

Chopsticks to fluff You can use a fork to gently 'fluff' rice before serving — that is, separate the grains — but an even gentler method is to use chopsticks, and as a bonus they don't scratch your pan.

 66 Get the pan right

It may sound obvious, but rice — and all grains, for that matter — will cook more evenly and end up with a far more consistent texture if the layer is not too thick in the pan. Also, make sure the pan is on a large enough heat source. If the water bubbles merrily at the centre of the pan but is placid around the edge, the heat source is too small.

 67 Treat it mean

With unpolished rice, such as brown and Camargue red, only the outermost layer — the hull — is removed during processing. This makes it more robust and much harder to ruin than white rice. It's not impossible, however. Perfectly cooked unpolished rice is tender but satisfyingly chewy and holds its shape; overcooked, it becomes unpleasantly swollen. Bring to the boil in plenty of water, then reduce the heat to a vigorous simmer. Cook for 35–40 minutes, until the rice is cooked but still has a bite, then drain off any excess water.

Leave it alone!
Resist the temptation to check the rice until it's rested off the heat for 5 minutes. Now you can peek!

 **3 Golden rules**

68 Cooking rice

1 Measure the rice by volume rather than weight (before soaking) and use one-and-one-third the volume of water to cook the rice.

2 Start cooking the rice in cold water — do not boil the water first. When the water comes to a boil, reduce the heat to the minimum and cover the pan with a tight-fitting lid. Cook for 20 minutes.

3 Remove the cooked rice from the heat, take off the lid and quickly place a clean tea towel over the pan. Return the lid and set aside for 5 minutes. The tea towel will absorb any steam and prevent it dripping back into the rice.

Rice ID

Most rice is multipurpose, with slightly different results in terms of taste and texture, but some dishes only work with the right type — you can't make successful sushi with basmati, for example, or paella with wild rice. Here is a guide to some well-known varieties from around the world. Cooking times apply to simmering after bringing to the boil.

Colour	Name	Characteristics	Where it is grown	Cooking time	Use for ...
White	Long-grain	Mild flavour, fluffy texture	U.S.	20 minutes	Side dish, fried rice, pilaf, salad, stuffing for vegetables and chicken
	Basmati	Long-grain, fragrant, tender	Himalayan foothills	30 minutes soaking; 10–12 minutes	Side dish, pilaf, stuffing for vegetables and chicken
	Jasmine	Long-grain, soft, slightly sticky	Thailand	18 minutes	Side dish, fried rice, stuffing for vegetables and chicken, rice pudding
	Risotto	Short- or medium-grain, releases starch on cooking	Italy	20 minutes	Risotto (see pages 52–53), stuffing for vegetables, rice pudding
	Paella	Short-grain, highly absorbent, retains shape and texture	Spain	20 minutes	Paella (see pages 54–55), rice pudding
	Sushi	Short-grain, firm, slightly gelatinous	Japan	18 minutes	Sushi (see pages 56–57)
Brown	Long-, medium- or short-grain	Unpolished, robust, chewy, nutty	U.S., Italy	45 minutes	Side dish, stuffing for vegetables and chicken, salad, soup
	Basmati	Fragrant, nutty, slightly chewy	Himalayan foothills	25 minutes	Side dish, stuffing for vegetables and chicken, salad, soup
Red	Camargue	Unpolished, firm, nutty, colourful	France	35–40 minutes	Side dish, risotto, stuffing for vegetables and chicken, salad, soup, rice pudding
Black	Venere	Medium-grain, mild nutty flavour, aromatic	Italy	35–40 minutes	Side dish, risotto (good with seafood), stuffing for vegetables and chicken, salad, soup, rice pudding
	Wild	Not technically rice, but a rice-shaped grass seed; chewy, nutty, sweet, smoky	Wild in U.S., Canada; grown around the world	45 minutes; seeds burst open when cooked	Side dish, salad, stuffing for vegetables and chicken, looks good partnered with other types of rice

Perfect risotto

Traditional risotto-making demands a generous half hour of your undivided attention, but the task is therapeutic and the rewards infinite — a dish that is elegant, flavourful, appealing and always comforting.

69 Simple risotto for two

1 Melt 25 g (1 oz) of butter or 1 tablespoon of olive oil in a straight-sided, heavy-bottomed pan. Add half a medium onion, finely chopped, and soften over low heat. Stir in the rice, allowing a handful of dried rice per person, as a rule of thumb.

70 The magic is in the rice

A great risotto starts with the right type of rice, which is grown mainly in the fertile plains of the Po river valley in northern Italy. Risotto rice is high in amylopectin, a starch that is released as you cook the rice, resulting in the characteristic creaminess of a risotto but leaving the grains satisfyingly al dente (firm). Stirring the rice constantly as it cooks coaxes the starch from the grains.

Arborio
The classic (and least expensive) risotto rice, with the highest level of amylopectin. Use this for any basic creamy risotto, such as mushroom.

Vialone nano
Short, plump grains with a lower level of amylopectin, favoured in the Veneto region. Use this for a robust risotto Milanese to serve with meat.

Carnaroli
Large, translucent grains with a good 'bite'. This delicate rice has a perfect balance of amylopectin and amylose, the starch that keeps the grains al dente on cooking. Carnaroli is considered the superior variety — use it to make a lighter, looser risotto.

Risotto rice has got an undeserved reputation for being tricky to cook: it isn't. It's one of the easiest of ingredients to prepare, and — depending on what you add to it — perfect for a winter feast or a light summer lunch.

2 When the rice is hot, add half a glass of white wine to the pan and stir the rice with a wooden spoon until the wine is absorbed. Then add hot stock one ladleful at a time, stirring constantly until the stock is almost absorbed before adding another ladleful. Keep adding stock until the rice is cooked and creamy but still retains a hint of bite.

3 This is the final stage. Remove the pan from the heat, add 25 g (1 oz) unsalted butter and 25 g (1 oz) freshly grated Parmesan, beat vigorously and serve immediately. And that's it, a delicious basic risotto! From here, you can add seasonal vegetables, chicken, seafood — whatever you have in the refrigerator.

TRY IT

Holey spoon A 'girosiro' is a wooden spoon with a large hole in the bowl, which effectively doubles your stirring power.

3 Golden rules   71

Cooking risotto

1 Use a well-flavoured chicken or vegetable stock. Bring 1.5 litres (2½ pints) of stock to a boil in a separate pan before you start cooking your risotto, then keep it at a rolling boil. It must be hot!

2 Don't let the grains brown when 'toasting' the rice (see step 1, above), as this will lock in the starch.

3 Reduce the amount of stock you add each time when the rice is starting to soften, to avoid overcooking.

FIX IT

Starchy risotto? If your risotto is more starchy than you'd like after adding the butter and Parmesan, simply loosen it with a little more hot stock. Bon appétit!

Embellish your dish Be sure to add another ingredient with texture to your risotto, to add contrast and visual interest.

TRY IT

Serve in style For a risotto that looks as good as it tastes, try any one of the following:
• Serve a spoonful of risotto in a grilled portobello mushroom as an appetizer.
• Bring a risotto to the table in a hollowed-out squash.
• Heap individual servings of risotto into halved grapefruit shells.

Balance the flavour
Use a combination of dried and fresh mushrooms in a risotto — dried pack more flavour punch, but too many can be overpowering.

5 Reasons **72**

to keep some risotto rice in your cupboard

1 Stuffed tomatoes, aubergine or peppers — cook risotto rice in broth without stirring, and add cheese, herbs and pine nuts.

2 Irresistible arancini — deep-fried risotto balls with melting mozzarella in the centre.

3 Venetian 'risi e bisi' (rice and peas) — a comforting soupy risotto without the stirring, perfect for weeknights.

4 Rice timbale — ragù encased in risotto set with eggs.

5 Naturally creamy rice pudding — add lemon zest for Italian zing.

RISOTTO FLAVOUR COMBOS

Transform your risotto into a culinary triumph with some interesting variations — replace the wine with champagne or vermouth, for example, or the Parmesan with a different cheese. Try the following combinations:

Champagne   poached egg   dill

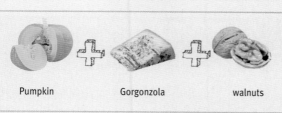

Pumpkin   Gorgonzola   walnuts

Red wine   beetroot   feta

3 Golden rules **73** Traditional paella

1 Keep it simple. Paella is all about the rice and the flavour you add to it. For a seafood paella, use a really well-flavoured fish stock (see page 25) and, ideally, Spanish saffron and pimentón.

2 Paella rice is shaken, not stirred, during cooking. When you add ingredients, give the frying pan a gentle shake, but that's all. The idea is for the rice on the bottom of the pan to cook undisturbed in order to form a deliciously crisp, caramelized crust called a *socarrat*.

3 Eat paella at room temperature rather than piping hot, and straight from the pan, as the Spanish do. No plates allowed!

74 The secret of the paella pan

An authentic paella pan is wide and shallow, allowing the rice to settle in a thin layer as it cooks (it should be no deeper than a finger's width), and has a thin base, which makes the highly prized socarrat easier to achieve. Budding paella addicts should definitely consider acquiring one!

Sunshine seafood paella

Paella, like risotto, is made with short-grain rice and a well-flavoured stock, but there the resemblance ends. The finest authentic Spanish paella rice is called *bomba*. The grains absorb more liquid (and flavour) than other rice varieties, but remain firm and separate, without either releasing starch or overcooking. *Calasparra* is an excellent — if marginally less exalted — alternative.

Ingredients

2 tbsp olive oil
1 onion, finely chopped
1 garlic clove, crushed
2 large, ripe tomatoes, skinned and chopped
2 tbsp fino sherry
1 tsp pimentón
200 g (7 oz) paella rice
400 ml fish stock
Pinch of saffron threads, soaked in warm water
400 g (14 oz) mixed seafood, e.g., white fish cut into chunks, mussels and prawns
Sliced chorizo (optional)
Handful of frozen petits pois, thawed

1 Heat a paella pan or wide frying pan, add the olive oil and sauté the onion, garlic and tomatoes. Add the sherry and cook until reduced to a purée. Add the pimentón and cook for 1 minute.
2 Stir in the rice, followed by the stock and the saffron water. Bring to a boil and simmer for 10 minutes.
3 Add your seafood of choice and the chorizo slices, if using. Shake the pan gently and cook for an additional 8–10 minutes, adding a little more stock if the rice starts to look dry but without drowning it.
4 Stir in the petits pois. Cover the pan with foil or a lid, remove from the heat and set aside for 10 minutes. Garnish with chopped flat-leaf parsley and lemon wedges.

Sensational sushi

Japan has captured the imagination of the Western world with beautiful, healthy sushi. A sushi chef trains for years in the art — the rest of us can only aspire, and have fun trying.

Nigiri

Maki

Uramaki

75 **It all starts with the rice ...**

Sushi rice is short-grained and slightly sticky when cooked — the stickiness is essential to form a firm mould for the other ingredients, and to ensure it doesn't escape from its *nori* wrapping. Japanese devotees to sushi use 'new-crop' rice, called *shinmai*. Outside Japan, the alternatives are *koshihikari*, *sasanishiki* and *akita komachi*. Another option — not authentic, but with very similar characteristics to the real deal — is Selenio rice from Italy.

76 Sushi rolls

To make sushi rolls, you need sheets of dried and toasted nori to hold the filling in place. A bamboo sushi mat is useful — and inexpensive — or you can improvise with aluminium foil or greaseproof paper.

1 Lay a nori sheet on the bamboo mat, with the shiny side down and the lines vertical.
2 Dampen your hands with water mixed with rice vinegar and lightly spread an even layer of rice over the nori, leaving a 2 cm (³/₄-inch) border at the top end.
3 Place your chosen fillings horizontally across the centre of the rice. Don't overdo it — less is more where elegant sushi is concerned.
4 Roll the mat away from you, pressing lightly as you roll. Remember to stop before you roll the mat into the sushi.
5 Hold the mat away to make the final roll. The filling should now be snuggled comfortably in the nori.

6 Transfer the roll to a cutting board and cut it in half. Place one half beside the other and cut both together into three rolls. You need a really sharp knife for this — a sashimi knife is ideal. Dip it in a rice vinegar and water mix before cutting.
7 Serve with bowls of wasabi, pickled ginger and soy sauce for dipping.

First is best
Be careful with rolling, as a re-roll will never be as successful as the first one.

77 Take your time

Sushi rice requires dedication. First, swish the rice briskly in several changes of water, until the water remains almost clear. Drain in a fine sieve for 1 hour before cooking. Once cooked and rested, fluff the rice with a rice paddle or wooden spatula and turn it out into a *hangiri* (a wooden rice bowl) or shallow non-metallic bowl. Now fan the rice energetically for 30 seconds with one hand, while turning it gently with the paddle in the other hand. Then sprinkle with the seasoned rice vinegar and continue to fan and paddle, lifting and folding to incorporate the seasoning, until the rice is at room temperature — about 5 minutes.

FIX IT

Alternative to rolling If your sushi rice is perfect but your rolling skills need work, make chirashi instead — scattered sushi. It's simply sushi rice in a bowl with the other ingredients scattered on top.

78 Sweet stuff

A good-quality commercial sushi seasoning is a combination of rice vinegar, soy sauce and mirin (sweetened rice wine). The best mirin is made with naturally sweet rice and contains no added sweeteners.

Sushi ID

Sushi comes in a variety of shapes and sizes, some easy to create, some far more intricate and best left to the experts. Here are a few of the best for the novice sushi chef to try:

Name	Meaning	Made from ...	Equipment
Temari	Ball	Rice, fish, garnish	Cling film
Chirashi	Scattered	Rice, seafood, vegetables, garnish	Serving bowl
Nigiri	Hand-formed	Rice, fish, garnish	Hands
Oshi	Pressed	Rice, fish, garnish	*Oshibako* (wooden press) or improvise with a shallow storage container lined with cling film
Maki	Rolled	Nori, rice, fish, vegetables	*Makisu* (bamboo sushi mat) or improvise with sturdy aluminium foil or greaseproof paper
Uramaki	Inside-out rolls	Nori, rice, fish, vegetables, coating	As for maki — if using a makisu, place it inside a plastic freezer bag to avoid a sticky mess

Pasta, bella!

Pasta, how do I describe thee? Let me count the ways … Light, filling, comforting, elegant — it can be whatever you want it to be, depending on season, sauce and shape.

79 Cooking fresh pasta

Fresh pasta, especially if filled, is an altogether more delicate thing than dried. It cooks very quickly, and once the water has come back to the boil after adding the pasta, it will cook perfectly at a rather more leisurely boil than dried pasta.

80 Why all the shapes?

Pasta comes in three basic types:
Long and smooth — spaghetti, tagliatelle
Short and solid — farfalle, radiatori
Hollow — penne, conchiglie.
The type of pasta you choose is influenced by the sauce you're serving with it. The two elements must be united, and the shape of the pasta — and whether it's smooth (*lisce*) or ridged (*rigate*) — needs consideration. It's all about trapping and clinging. See the ID chart opposite for clues.

81 Plenty of salted boiling water …

Instructions for cooking dried pasta always start with a large pan of salted boiling water — enough water that the individual pasta strands or shapes can move freely once they are rehydrated. Too little water and you have a clump of pasta that's reluctant to come apart, although the addition of more water (boiling — never add cold) and a lot of stirring sometimes helps. And salt? Also a lot — as the saying goes, enough to make the water taste like the sea. This enhances the flavour of the pasta, but doesn't overwhelm it (or you) with salt. Add once the water is boiling.

5 Reasons 82

to keep a packet of penne in your cupboard

1 Penne is a classic partner for the ragù sauce you keep in the freezer (see page 61).

2 Ribbed penne's great for a chunky, robust sauce — the sauce clings to the ridges on the outside and the slanted ends lure the sauce into the hollow centre.

3 If you crave macaroni and cheese but have no macaroni, penne makes a passable substitute.

4 Penne retains its shape well for serving 'al forno' (baked).

5 Penne's a perfect size and has a really good 'bite' for pasta salads.

FIX IT

Firming flabby Dried pasta seems fairly robust, but overcook it for even a couple of minutes and you'll have a panful of flabby pasta with a very unpleasant mouthfeel. Your only chance of reprieve is to drain the pasta immediately, rinse it under cold running water (which otherwise never do, except for pasta salads), then warm it gently in its sauce.

TRY IT

Holey insert If you struggle with draining a heavy pot of pasta, consider investing in a perforated pasta insert. It fits inside an ordinary pot (make sure the sizes are compatible!) and when the pasta is cooked you simply lift up the insert, leaving the water in the pan.

Pasta ID

The tally of pasta shapes runs into the hundreds. Here's a list of a mere handful of them, to give you an idea of how to make your pasta and sauce compatible. The general idea is that light sauces go with light pasta, and robust sauces go with thick or ribbed pasta.

	Name	Type	Characteristics	Sauce
	Spaghetti	Strand	Long, thin, cylindrical; world's most popular pasta	Light, e.g., garlic and oil, puttanesca, carbonara, pesto
	Bucatini	Strand	Similar to spaghetti but thicker and with a hollow centre	Robust, e.g., amatriciana, anchovy
	Fusilli	Strand	Short strands, twisted into spirals	Robust, e.g., lentil, amatriciana
	Linguine	Ribbon	Similar to spaghetti but flattened	Light, e.g., tomato, vongole (clam)
	Tagliatelle	Ribbon	Flat, wide, not quite straight	Robust, e.g., ragù, radicchio/cream/ham
	Fettucine	Ribbon	Slightly wider, thicker version of tagliatelle	Light, e.g., Alfredo
	Penne	Tubular	Cylindrical, cut on a slant, smooth or ribbed	Robust, e.g., ragù, amatriciana
	Tortiglioni	Tubular	Chunky, slanted grooves	Robust, e.g., sausage, lentil, courgette
	Farfalle	Solid	Butterfly-shaped with frilled wings	Light, e.g., pesto, prosciutto/cream
	Radiatori	Solid	Radiator-shaped with deep grooves for trapping sauce	Robust, e.g., radicchio/cream/ham
	Conchiglie	Hollow	Shells with ribbed outside and smooth interior, great for chunks of sauce to hide in	Light, e.g., arrabiata, and robust vegetable, e.g., broccoli, broad bean/ricotta

3
Golden
rules

83

Cooking dried pasta

1 Make sure the water is boiling briskly before adding dried pasta, and cook it at a vigorous boil.

2 Check the guidelines for specific cooking times, which vary depending on the type of pasta. Pasta takes only a few minutes to cook and the time passes quickly, so set a timer to go off before the end of the recommended cooking time.

3 Test the pasta when the timer goes off — it should always remain al dente (and needs to be on the underdone side if you're using the pasta in a bake, as it will be cooked further in the oven). When it's cooked to perfection, remove the pot from the heat and drain the pasta immediately to arrest the cooking.

Serious about sauce

Pasta needs sauce. It doesn't need to be complicated but it needs to be there. A freshly made pesto, a simple carbonara or the ultimate in pasta sauce heaven — a rich, aromatic ragù.

84 Save water!

Pasta water is salty, cloudy with released starch and a magic ingredient in sauces, so always save a little before draining the pasta. It's useful for 'loosening' a sauce you've already made, or you can simply toss pasta in a naturally creamy sauce made from warmed olive oil or butter (or both) and a splash of pasta water — the fat and liquid emulsify (see page 154) like French dressing. Add freshly grated Parmesan and dinner's ready!

85 Give us a twirl

Spaghetti carbonara is simple yet stunning, just the job for a weeknight. While the spaghetti is cooking, sauté 150 g (5 oz) cubed pancetta in 2 tablespoons olive oil until crisp but still meltingly tender. Add a splash of white wine if you like. Beat 4 eggs with 2 egg yolks and add 90 g (3 oz) finely grated cheese (⅔ Pecorino, ⅓ Parmesan). Season with black pepper. Drain the spaghetti, then toss it in the pan with the pancetta. Turn off the heat, add the egg mixture and toss again, thoroughly — the heat of the pasta cooks the eggs and melts the cheese. Add a splash of pasta water. Serve in deep bowls — twirl it in with pasta tongs, then lift it and give it an extra twirl. This is not essential to the success of the dish — but it looks so much prettier than a dollop! Sprinkle with Parmesan.

TRY IT

Pasta tongs Useful for all your pasta manipulation needs, pasta tongs are an Italian kitchen must-have, from fishing out a strand of spaghetti to test that it's done (it's annoyingly elusive with a fork) to serving and twirling.

PESTO FLAVOUR COMBOS

Pesto is traditionally made with basil, Parmesan and pine nuts, but the following combinations are also divine:

Watercress   Parmesan   almonds

lemon

Cavolo nero   Pecorino   walnuts

Rocket   Parmesan   hazelnuts

orange zest

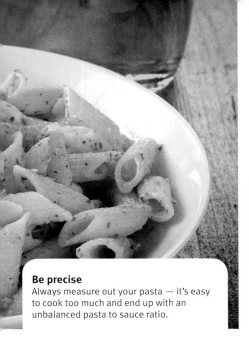

86 Room to swirl

The ideal pan for cooking any sort of pasta sauce is a wide, deep sauté pan. Drain the pasta while it's still slightly too al dente and toss it in the pan with the sauce (remember to add some of the pasta water). In one fell swoop, the sauce will finish cooking the pasta and cling to it evenly and tenaciously.

5 Reasons 87

to keep ragù in your freezer

1 Serve with tagliatelle or penne as a classic pasta Bolognese.

2 Use as a ravioli filling (reduce the ragù until firm).

3 Combine with pasta sheets and cheese sauce to make lasagne.

4 Stuff vegetables — aubergine, peppers, tomatoes — and bake in the oven.

5 Use with leftover risotto to make *arancini con ragù* (rice balls stuffed with meat sauce).

Classic ragù

Ragù needs a long, slow cooking time to mature to a rich depth, so it's worth making a huge batch and freezing some.

Ingredients
50 g (1¾ oz) butter or 3 tbsp olive oil
50 g (1¾ oz) pancetta, finely chopped
1 carrot, finely chopped
1 stick of celery, finely chopped
1 onion, finely chopped
1 anchovy (optional)
100 g (3½ oz) lean beef mince
100 g (3½ oz) lean pork mince
6 tbsp red wine
3 tbsp tomato paste
Beef or chicken stock

1 Melt the butter, add the pancetta, carrot, celery and onion and gently sauté for 10 minutes to soften. This is a good moment to sneak in an anchovy, too, for added umami.
2 Stir in the beef and pork and cook for 15 minutes until browned. If you want to mince the meat yourself, the technique is given on page 33.
3 Add the red wine, cook for 3 minutes, then add the tomato paste (try a sun-dried one for a really intense flavour) followed by a splash or two of good beef or chicken stock (see pages 35 and 45) — enough to prevent the meat from sticking.
4 Simmer for at least 1½ hours — more if you like — adding more stock as necessary. Season to taste.

Artisan pasta

Homemade pasta dough is surprisingly easy and there's a rewarding element of fun to the process. There are also endless creative opportunities, both in flavouring the pasta and in the way you use it.

A helping hand
Guide the pasta out of the shaping attachment to prevent it landing in a tangled heap.

3 Golden rules

88 Pasta dough

1 Rest the pasta dough in a cool place for an hour before rolling to relax the gluten in the flour. This makes the dough easier to work with.

2 Use fine semolina or polenta for rolling out and resting the shaped pasta. If you use flour for rolling out, the dough absorbs it, making it difficult to work with, and if you rest the shaped pasta on flour it turns to glue and welds the pasta together as it cooks. Semolina keeps its distance.

3 Let the pasta dough dry out a little on a dusting of semolina before shaping, and let the shapes dry out before cooking or storing or they'll stick together in an unmanageable blob. A pasta stand is useful for keeping long strands separate; the back of a chair also does the trick.

89 Fine flours

Pasta flour — look for the words 'Type 00' on the packaging — is very fine and silky. It's made from hard durum wheat, which has a high protein and gluten content. You can also experiment with other types of flour — spelt works well, or a mix of 00 and chestnut flour or buckwheat flour. A mix of 00 and semolina results in a grainy 'bite', which is good for ravioli.

90 Pasta machine

All you really need for pasta making is a rolling pin and a sharp knife, but a pasta machine does make the job easier. The rollers complete the kneading as you pass the dough through repeatedly and of course you end up with a uniformly thin dough. And although you can simply roll up the dough and cut it into strips, it's far more entertaining to watch tagliatelle and linguine emerging from the shaping attachment.

91 DIY dough

A little goes a long way with homemade pasta. Experiment with 100 g (3½ oz) of flour and one room-temperature egg. You can make the dough in a food processor — process the ingredients until they resemble breadcrumbs, then turn the mixture out and knead it — but to be a true artisan, mix it by hand.

1 Sift the flour into a mound and make a well in the centre. Sprinkle a little fine salt over the top. Break the egg into the well.

2 This part is messy! With one finger, stir the egg briskly to break it up. Start drawing in the flour, a little at a time, then as it thickens use all your fingers to draw it all together.

3 Knead for 5 minutes, until the dough feels smooth and silky, adding a little olive oil if the dough is too dry or extra flour if too wet. It should feel firm and robust.

TRY IT

Build an open lasagne A traditional lasagne is hearty, but an open lasagne, made with thin homemade pasta, is light. Have the filling ready to assemble when you cook the pasta. Drain the pasta and drizzle with olive oil. Arrange one sheet on a plate, spoon over some filling, fold a second sheet of pasta artistically on top and top with more filling. Cut circles out of the lasagne using a cookie cutter for an elegant starter.

92 Rolling your dough

Scatter fine semolina or polenta on a cutting board and roll out half the dough into a rectangle (keep the other half covered in cling film). Fold the short ends in and roll again. Do this three times. Now feed it through the pasta machine with the rollers on the widest setting. Put the dough through 10 times on this setting, folding each time. Progressively reduce the width setting to the second-finest (the finest is usually a step too far), passing the dough through once each time. As the dough stretches, flip the emerging end back over the top of the machine or it will concertina and stick.

93 Fancy flavourings

Now that you have the know-how to make a basic egg pasta, it's time to get creative! You can add colour and flavour with vegetable purée (spinach is a classic, but also try butternut squash or beetroot — make sure the purée is really dry), sun-dried tomato paste, dried and ground porcini mushrooms, saffron powder, unsweetened cocoa powder or chopped herbs. You might need to tweak the liquid — try using a small egg for a moist flavouring or a large egg for a powdered one.

94 Pretty pasta

Before you shape the dough, brush it with egg white and scatter soft herb leaves and edible flowers over one half, lengthways. Fold over the other half, trim the edges and run the dough through the rollers once on the second-finest setting. Avoid herbs and flowers with spiky stalks, as these will puncture the dough.

Adding flavour
Stir a spoonful of pesto into the pasta dough with the egg and add a little extra flour if necessary.

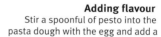
95 Shaping ravioli

Filled pasta is fun to make and satisfying to eat. The easiest is ravioli, which you can shape by hand or in a mould.

By hand
1 Roll out the pasta into a long strip and cut it in half lengthways. Spoon mounds of filling at intervals along one half, and lay the other half on top.

2 Cut out the shapes using a ravioli stamp, pastry cutter, fluted pastry wheel or a sharp knife — the last two methods are useful for making larger or even giant ravioli. Press out the air around the filling (see Three Golden Rules).

Ravioli mould By using a mould, you're less likely to end up with air pockets around the filling. The technique varies with the type of mould, but the idea is that you lay a sheet of pasta over the mould, press it gently into the pockets (some moulds come with a shaping press), add your filling to the pockets, lay another sheet of pasta over the top and seal with a rolling pin. Then you simply turn out the ravioli, dry for an hour or so on a tray sprinkled with semolina and cook.

TRY IT

Chocolate pasta This sounds like a weird concept, but it's really good! Chocolate pasta works well with strong umami flavours such as smoked salmon, mushrooms or feta cheese — but who says pasta dishes have to be savoury? Try ravioli with a filling of mascarpone and sweetened chestnut purée and top with a drizzle of cream and chilli chocolate curls.

RAVIOLI FLAVOUR COMBOS

Herbed pasta enhances the flavour and appearance of ravioli. You can chop the herbs, but whole leaves and edible flowers look really appealing. Try these combinations:

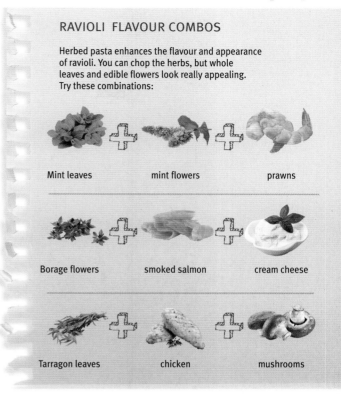

Mint leaves   mint flowers   prawns

Borage flowers   smoked salmon   cream cheese

Tarragon leaves   chicken   mushrooms

3 Golden rules

96 Successful ravioli

1 Brush the bottom sheet of pasta all over with beaten egg white before arranging the mounds of filling. This anchors the filling in place and seals the pasta layers.

2 Use a filling with a firm, dry consistency. It's easier to control and less inclined to escape during cooking.

3 Always carefully press out the air before sealing the two layers of pasta. Air trapped around the filling tends to expand, causing the pasta to burst while it is cooking.

Plump little parcels
The serrated edges on ravioli aren't just for decoration — they actually help seal the pasta.

97 Brown butter

Filled pasta is wonderful served with a drizzle of brown butter. Heat a heavy-based frying pan over medium-high heat, add the butter and stir constantly for about 2 minutes, until the butter turns a hazelnut colour — but no darker. The trick is to use unsalted butter, which is slower to burn than salted. Sizzle whole or torn sage leaves in the butter towards the end of cooking and, if you like, add some toasted nuts for an irresistible crunch.

TRY IT

Catch your pasta! Filled pasta is too fragile to drain in a colander — use a large slotted spoon to lift it carefully out of the water.

Know your noodle

What's the difference between pasta and noodles? Pasta is the Italian product made from durum wheat, whereas noodles are Asian and made from all sorts of flours. That's how it works, more or less …

98 The Western noodle

Noodles aren't exclusively Asian — in fact, the word derives from the German *nudel*. *Spätzle* is a German egg noodle served tossed in butter as a side dish. To experiment, beat 1 egg with 4 tablespoons of milk and stir the mixture into 60 g (2 oz) plain flour (seasoned with salt) to make a thick batter. To cook the Spätzle, squish the batter through the holes of a colander into a pan of simmering water. When the noodles rise to the surface (2–4 minutes), resembling chubby little dumplings, they're done. Dedicated Spätzle fans use a special gadget for squishing.

Drunken noodles

There's nothing in this dish to induce drunkness, apart from the rice wine en route to being vinegar — it just seems to be universally loved.

Ingredients
250 g (9 oz) rice noodles
8 tsp fish sauce
8 tsp soy sauce
8 tsp rice wine vinegar
8 tsp light brown sugar
4 tbsp rapeseed oil
2 onions, chopped
4 garlic cloves, crushed
8 Thai chillies, diagonally sliced
400 g (14 oz) raw prawns
100 g (4 oz) vegetables, e.g., broccoli, peas, peppers
Lime wedges, to serve

1 Soak the rice noodles according to the instructions on the packet. Meanwhile, stir together the fish sauce, soy sauce, rice wine vinegar and light brown sugar.
2 Heat the rapeseed oil in a wok or frying pan over medium heat and stir-fry the onions, crushed garlic and chillies. Stir until the chillies make your eyes water.
3 Drain the noodles and add to the pan with the fish sauce mixture. Add the prawns and vegetables and stir-fry until the prawns are pink and tender and the veggies just wilted. Garnish with lime wedges.

Perfect prawns
The prawns add sweetness to this spicy dish, but they can be replaced easily with your meat of choice — chicken, beef or pork all work well.

Noodle ID

Asian noodles are not as ornate as pasta — their diversity lies instead in their thickness. The more robust types are made from wheat or buckwheat, whereas the delicate varieties are mostly derived from ingredients such as rice or mung beans.

	Name	From	Made with ...	Characteristics	How to prepare	Ways to serve ...
	Soba	Japan	Wheat/buckwheat	Robust, chewy, nutty	Boil	Cold with dipping sauce, soups, salads, stir-fries
	Cha soba	Japan	Wheat/buckwheat/green tea powder	Robust, chewy, delicate flavour	Boil	Do as the Japanese and save for special occasions
	Udon	Japan	Wheat	Robust, chewy	Boil	Stir-fries, soups, cold with dipping sauce
	Somen	Japan	Wheat	White, very thin	Boil	Cold with dipping sauce, soups
	Ramen	Japan	Wheat	White, robust, chewy	Boil	Soups, salads, stir-fries
	Egg	China	Wheat	Robust, chewy; variety of thicknesses	Boil	Stir-fries, chow mein
	Cellophane/glass	Throughout Asia	Mung bean starch	Glossy, translucent, gelatinous	Soak	Soups, salads, spring rolls
	Glass	Korea	Sweet potato starch	Glossy, translucent, chewy	Soak	*Japchae*
	Vermicelli	Throughout Asia	Rice	White, opaque, bland	Soak	In sweet rice wine vinegar dressing

99 Read the instructions

Asian noodles are so diverse in character that there's no 'one size fits all' instruction for cooking them — for example, somen noodles are boiled for 2 minutes, udon for 10 minutes and cellophane noodles are just soaked in hot water — so remember to check the guidelines on the packet. And if they advise you to 'drain then rinse under cold running water' after cooking, remember to do the rinsing bit or you'll have a solid noodle block.

A handful of grains

Rice and pasta are comforting because they're familiar. We understand their capabilities. But the world is full of grains — and things with grain aspirations — that can be embraced as alternatives.

Textured sponge
Use fine polenta for cakes — it adds a lovely texture without being too grainy.

101 Polenta — work it

Polenta is the (rather more lyrical) Italian name for cornmeal. It's easy to cook but rather bland, so it needs strong flavours — vegetable broth, butter, cheese (Parmesan is ideal), herbs (rosemary works), garlic, grated lemon zest — at which point it's miraculously transformed into deliciousness.

102 Traditional polenta cooking method

Use five times the volume of salted water or stock to polenta. Bring the liquid to the boil then turn the heat to its lowest setting. Remove the pan from the heat and slowly add the polenta (pouring it from a jug is easiest), stirring constantly. Return to the heat and cook for about 45 minutes, stirring occasionally with a wooden spoon. When it's cooked, it pulls away from the sides of the pan.

5 Reasons 100 to keep some polenta in your cupboard

1 Cook up a big batch, using half as a creamy accompaniment and letting the rest firm up to griddle or fry in wedges the next day.

2 Replace a pastry tart crust with polenta — line a tart pan with cooked polenta and bake it until dry and crisp before adding the filling.

3 Polenta can be used instead of semolina for rolling out and resting pasta.

4 Make polenta cake — it works really well with oranges, and it's equally good with chocolate.

5 Add polenta to biscuits and cookies for extra crunch and texture.

103 Health and safety warning!

If you pour the polenta directly into boiling water, it splatters alarmingly and you run the risk of burning yourself. By removing the pan from the heat to add the polenta and returning it to the very lowest setting, the most you see is a cursory bubble. The polenta cooks slowly, sedately and perfectly and only requires a quick stir every couple of minutes.

104 Polenta wedges

Creamy, just-cooked polenta undergoes a personality change when it cools — it firms up after about 30 minutes in the refrigerator and you can cut it into wedges (or squares, or blocks) and fry them until crisp and golden.

1 Make the polenta thick enough to hold its shape in the pan then add a little butter and cheese, chopped herbs and seasoning.

2 Pour into a greased shallow heat-proof dish and smooth the top with a knife (dip the knife in oil to make this easier).

3 When firm, turn out the polenta onto a cutting board and cut it into wedges. Fry in a little olive oil and/or butter for 3–5 minutes on each side until golden.

TRY IT

Spurtle This Scottish round-ended wooden stick designed to prevent lumpy porridge is also perfect for preventing lumpy polenta (and handy for keeping grains on the move as you're 'toasting' them; see page 71).

Happiness on a plate
Bitter chicory, sweet lettuce, crisp baby broad beans, chewy halloumi cheese and crunchy polenta fingers. What more could you want?

105 There's more to otto than ris

There are two grains that make an excellent substitute for rice in a risotto — spelt and barley (although risotto, by virtue of its name, is made with rice, the dishes made with these grains must therefore be called speltotto and barleyotto, respectively). Both grains are sold 'pearled' — that is, with the outer husk removed. They are more robust than risotto rice, and take rugged, cold-weather ingredients really well — kale, dried porcini mushrooms, chestnuts. And they're more self-sufficient, too — you can get away with less stirring, useful if you're short on time. What's not to love?

Pearl barley

Quinoa

106 Handling quinoa

Quinoa (pronounced 'keen-wah') is a pseudo-cereal, newly trendy beyond its native Andes. It comes in white, red and black varieties — cook separately and combine after cooking for a striking effect. It's very easy to end up with soggy quinoa. Here's how not to. You'll need exactly double the volume of water to quinoa.

1 Rinse the quinoa thoroughly under cold running water to remove the bitter coating from the seeds.
2 Heat a pan over medium-high heat and add a drizzle of olive oil.

3 Add the quinoa and stir until just dry and toasted. You can hear as much as see when this happens.
4 Add the water and season with salt, or use stock to add flavour. Bring to the boil, then immediately turn the heat to low. Cover and cook for 15 minutes.
5 Remove from the heat and set aside, still covered, for 5 minutes, then fluff with a fork (you'll see that each grain now has a little white halo, where the germ has separated from the kernel during cooking). If you're planning to use the quinoa in a salad, let it cool uncovered to dry out.

107 Not just for the birds

Millet is a grain, largely alien to the Western world except as a treat for caged birds — but it's actually delicious, with a bit of help. Rinse the millet thoroughly and cook as you would quinoa, but use three times the volume of water, and let it stand, covered, for 20 minutes after cooking. This keeps the grains separate (perfect for burgers, with veggies or in a salad), but if you stir in butter and cheese before serving, the millet takes on a creamy risotto-like texture. Millet benefits from strong flavours — cook it in a good vegetable or chicken stock, or add garlic and herbs.

Millet

108 No wheat in buckwheat

Buckwheat is neither a wheat nor a grain, but a small seed. Buckwheat flour is used to make soba noodles, and works well in pancakes, especially blinis — yeasted pancakes. The hulled seeds, or groats, are delicious toasted, when they're called 'kasha'. You can buy them ready-toasted, or do it yourself — either way, toasted buckwheat gives a better result when it's cooked. Toast it in a dry pan over a medium heat for 5 minutes, shaking the pan occasionally. Remove from the heat and add double the volume of boiling water, then return to the heat, covered, and simmer gently for 15–20 minutes until the water is absorbed.

109 Toasting — what's the point?

Toasting grains enhances their flavour and also regulates their absorption of liquid, so the grains end up fabulously fluffy, not depressingly damp. 'Toasting' is just the name of the technique, however, so aim to keep the grain the same colour as when it hit the pan. If it's toast colour, you've overdone it.

Buckwheat

Take your pick
You can make tabbouleh with bulgur wheat, quinoa or even couscous — try one made from barley for a change.

110 The lightest couscous

In its simplest form, couscous needs very little cooking — a quick soak in boiling water, add some butter and it's done. But in its native North Africa, they take the process more seriously, soaking it in cold water, aerating it frequently with oiled fingers (it's a messy job) then steaming it in a 'couscoussier', often above the fragrant stew it's to be served with. Finally, melted butter is worked into the couscous by hand. The result is really light — far better than the quick method. In the absence of a couscoussier, line an ordinary steamer basket with muslin.

TRY IT

Quinoa tabbouleh Quinoa makes a flavourful, chewy alternative to the traditional bulgur wheat in a Middle Eastern tabbouleh, a delectable summer dish made from industrial quantities of flat-leaf parsley along with mint leaves, juicy tomatoes and spring onions or shallots, held together with a hint of grain and dressed in olive oil, lemon juice and allspice. The key to a top-notch tabbouleh is to slice rather than cross-chop the herbs, to prevent bruising.

Luscious legumes

'Legumes' is the collective name for beans and lentils that are dried after they're harvested and rehydrated before they're eaten. They come in a glorious range of shapes, colours and uses.

FIX IT

Salvage mushy beans So you wandered off and forgot the beans were on the stove ... Overcooked beans lose their shape and texture, making them unappetizing in hearty bean soups and casseroles or salads, for example. But as long as they're not too far gone you can purée them into dips, or crush them into patties or bakes.

111 Why cheating is OK

Tinned beans are a shortcut that's occasionally worth taking. For starters, you don't have to remember to soak them. There's no danger of toxins — they've been destroyed for you. And finally, beans take ages to cook, so for small quantities it's almost certainly more efficient to buy them tinned. Brands vary, so try to find one where the beans are tender but with a good bite, not disintegrating.

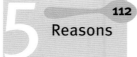

5 Reasons 112 to keep a tin of beans in your cupboard

1 Add to homemade ragù (see page 61) with a pinch of dried chilli flakes for a quick and easy chilli.

2 Mix with whole-grain rice, leaves, herbs and an oil-and-vinegar dressing to make a perfectly balanced salad. Try brown rice with borlotti beans, red rice with black beans or black rice with flageolet beans. Pretty!

3 Crush with sautéed onions, garlic, mushrooms, whatever you have, to make veggie burgers.

4 Add to a rustic vegetable soup and top with gremolata (see page 99).

5 Purée them into a dip — use any bean you like, but only call it 'hummus' if you use chickpeas (*hummus* means chickpeas in Arabic). Anything else is just dip. Try using nut butter instead of tahini, or a different seed butter. Experiment!

Beans ID

Dried beans are a staple food in many cultures around the world — they are, after all, an excellent way to preserve fresh beans. With the exception of black-eyed peas, they all need to be rehydrated before cooking, and some need longer than others.

	Name	Soaking time	Cooking time	Good for ...
	Red kidney beans	12 hours	1 hour	Chilli
	Black beans	12 hours	1–1½ hours	Chilli, refried beans, stews, dips
	Pinto beans	12 hours	1–1½ hours	Refried beans
	Haricot beans	8 hours	1–1½ hours	Baked beans, cassoulet
	Borlotti beans	8 hours	1–1½ hours	Salads, stews, minestrone
	Butter beans	8 hours	1–1½ hours	Soups, stews, mashed potatoes, Greek beans
	Cannellini beans	8 hours	1–1½ hours	Tuscan bean soup
	Flageolet beans	8 hours	1–1¼ hours	Salads, side dishes with cream and herbs
	Black-eyed peas	No soaking needed	1 hour	Rice and peas
	Adzuki beans	8 hours	1 hour	Red bean paste, salads
	Chickpeas	12 hours	1½ hours	Hummus, falafel, stews

Cover with water
Put plenty of water
in the pan when you
cook beans — after
soaking them for hours,
the last thing you want is
to burn them for want of a
few inches of H2O!

113   ## Cooking beans

**Golden
rules**

1 Rehydrate the beans
(see chart opposite
for soaking times) in
plenty of cold water before cooking. Cook the beans
in fresh water.

2 Add salt to both the soaking and cooking water —
the beans cook faster and the skins end up tender
but intact.

3 Boil hard for 10 minutes — red kidney beans are the
worst culprit for the toxin phytohemagglutinin, but it's
present to a lesser extent in other varieties, and it's
better to be safe than sorry. After this, lower the heat
to a steady simmer for the rest of the cooking time
(so you can see the beans jiggling around, but
nothing more).

114   ## How to avoid
bullet beans

You can soak beans, cook them for hours and they can
still end up hard. The problem might be the age of the
beans — they go stale with storage, sometimes to
the point where soaking has no impact. If your beans
have been lurking in the cupboard for longer than a
year, ditch them and get a new packet. Acid inhibits
softening, so if your recipe features a very acidic
ingredient, such as tomatoes, it's best to precook the
beans and reduce the cooking time, or add them at a
later stage of cooking.

Homemade Boston baked beans

Baked beans were the traditional Sunday fare for
early Boston settlers, served with steamed raisin
bread — so ditch the tins, and make them yourself.

Ingredients
450 g (16 oz) dried haricot beans
25 g (2 oz) soft brown sugar
6 tbsp blackstrap molasses
1 tbsp mustard powder
1/2 tsp freshly ground black pepper
4 cloves
2 small onions, peeled
350 g (12 oz) rindless salt pork
6 tbsp rum (optional)

1 Soak the beans and then cook in fresh water
until just tender. Drain the beans, saving the
cooking water, and transfer to a large ovenproof
casserole dish.
2 Stir in the soft brown sugar, blackstrap molasses,
mustard powder and black pepper.
3 Stick 2 cloves in each of the onions and add to
the beans.
4 Score the fat on the salt pork and push into the
beans. Add the cooking water and more water as
necessary to cover the beans.
5 Bake, covered, at 140°C (275°F) for 3 hours.
Remove the lid, lift the pork to the surface (and,
if you're feeling a bit wild, add rum) and cook for
a further hour to brown the fat.

115 ## Puy — the lentil king

Puy lentils are small, speckled and heavenly. They're named after the region in France where they're produced and are so superior in quality that they carry an AOC (Appellation d'Origine Contrôlée) — a lentil cannot call itself a genuine 'Puy' unless it comes from here. They cook in 20–25 minutes, retain their 'bite' and soak up flavours, so are wonderful in salads, where they are the star. It seems an insult to cast them in a lesser role.

Protein feast
Serving a lentil ragù with a grain, such as flatbread, makes a complete protein — great for vegetarians.

116 ## Lentil types

Lentils have major advantages over dried beans — there's no need to pre-soak them, no risk of toxin poisoning and they only take around 20–30 minutes to cook, depending on the type. Just rinse, drain and cook in three times their volume of unsalted water. There are basically two types of lentil — those that disintegrate when cooked, and those that don't.

Split lentils These cook in 20 minutes and quickly disintegrate. Split red lentils are great in spicy blended soups (try the Middle Eastern combo of lentil, dried apricot and cumin), and are particularly good with spices, garlic and chilli in an Indian dal.

Green, brown and black lentils These vary slightly in size, but are all essentially small. They are more inclined to keep their shape when cooked so are very versatile, adding texture and helping a little go a long way. You can add them raw to dishes cooked slowly in liquid, such as casseroles.

117 ## Lentil ragù

Vegetarian lentil ragù is as versatile as the meaty version. Use it in pasta dishes, to stuff vegetables, with creamy polenta or top it with mashed potatoes and cheese and bake it for rainy-day comfort. Replace the meat with Puy or Italian *Castelluccio* lentils as they hold their shape so well, and add some finely chopped chestnut mushrooms for their colour and flavour. And don't be stingy with the red wine!

Known by colour
With a few exceptions, lentils are identified by colour rather than name — thus, these are simply known as red, green and yellow lentils.

FROM THE GROUND

Fruits of the earth, nature's bounty, call them what you will — the edible plants that emerge from the soil add colour, flavour, texture and most of all joy to cooking. In this chapter, we look at ways to prepare, cook and innovate with these obliging culinary treasures from the ground.

Chopping, slicing, peeling

The prospect of preparing fruits and vegetables can be daunting, but equipment and technique make all the difference between making the most of plant food and settling for the occasional banana.

118   Under the knife

A medium or large all-purpose kitchen knife is perfect for chopping and slicing fruits and vegetables when appearance doesn't matter too much. The smallest size, with a 5 cm (2-inch) blade, is ideal for chopping finely — the shorter, narrower blade gives you better control over this more delicate operation.

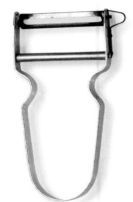

119   Why own a Y peeler?

A Y peeler is a gem of a gizmo, not only for peeling fruits and vegetables thinly and with very little waste, but also as a substitute for a mandoline — its limitation being the width of the blade. It's excellent for making fine strips or slices of slender vegetables such as carrots, courgette and cucumber. Peel carrots first, but leave the skin on courgette and cucumber. For added interest, try mixing purple or yellow carrots with orange ones, and yellow or striped courgette with green ones. Then simply run the peeler along the length or width of the vegetable. The Y peeler is also the perfect tool for making 'shavings' of hard cheese.

120   The rolling chop

The fastest way to slice most vegetables is with the technique known as the rolling chop. 'Rolling' describes the rocking, almost circular action of the knife. Remember to move your fingers as you progress along the vegetable. You'll speed up with practice!

Anchor the ingredient by making a 'claw' with one hand. With the tip resting on the cutting board, pull the knife back and down towards the ingredient, then slice through it, at the same time moving the knife forwards so it's in position to repeat the action.

121 Not the musical instrument

Meticulous cooks use a mandoline for slicing and making
julienne strips. A good mandoline has a choice of blades
and width settings, enabling you to make straight,
crinkle-cut or waffle slices and thick or thin julienne strips.
Although a bit of a chore to use until you get the hang of it,
once mastered the mandoline works particularly well for
robust vegetables such as onions, fennel, artichokes,
beetroot and cabbage — the ones that doggedly resist
your efforts to achieve uniformity.

Mandoline marvels
Ideal for thin slicing when
your knife skills fall short, a
mandoline can help improve
the presentation of your dishes.

122 Keep it fresh

Cutting into a fruit or vegetable damages its cells, triggering
a process called 'oxidation', which turns some fruits and
veggies a very unappetizing brown. When preparing apples,
pears, bananas, peaches, potatoes, aubergine or artichokes,
drop the chopped or sliced pieces immediately
into a bowl of acidulated water, made
by adding 2 teaspoons of lemon or
lime juice or vinegar (wine or
cider) to 1 litre of water.
A vitamin C tablet
works, too.

Act quickly
Drain and use potatoes as
soon as possible, as oxidation
starts the process of depleting
nutrients and taste, and
soaking continues it.

Root veggies

Root vegetables are exactly that — the edible roots of certain plants. Carrots, parsnips, celeriac, turnips and beetroot all qualify as roots.

123 Naturally sweet

The reason roasted root vegetables are so delectably crisp and brown is that they are rich in natural sugars, which caramelize on the surface in the heat of the oven — a process called 'the Maillard reaction' in scientific circles. Using your hands, coat the prepared vegetables thinly, but thoroughly and evenly, in olive oil — messy, but effective. Roast them in a moderately hot oven (200°C/400°F) for about 45 minutes until they're crisp and brown on the outside and meltingly soft inside. If you want to include onions (not strictly a root, but a bulb), add them halfway through cooking — they cook faster than, for example, carrots and parsnips.

3 Golden rules

124 Caramelizing veggies

1 **Cut vegetables into same-sized pieces** so they roast evenly. Too much variation and the smaller pieces will burn before the larger ones caramelize.

2 **Dry vegetable pieces with kitchen paper before coating in oil.** This helps to avoid creating steam in the oven and makes the caramelizing process faster and more efficient.

3 **Arrange vegetables in a single layer on a baking tray** — pile in too many and they'll steam rather than caramelize.

125 Glam glazing

A really attractive presentation technique for carrots and beetroot, the aim of glazing is to coat the veggies in melted butter, so they look glossy and appetizing. Steam carrots until al dente, then toss in a pan with butter — add flavourings if you like, such as orange zest and chopped herbs, and season with salt and pepper. Steam beetroot whole until almost cooked, peel when cool enough to handle, cut into wedges and finish off in the oven with butter and caraway seeds or sprigs of thyme, basting frequently. Glazing works well with other colourful veggies, too, such as green beans and butternut squash.

Herb it up
Throw in some 'woody' herbs when you're roasting veggies — sprigs of rosemary, thyme or lavender, or a few sage leaves.

Root veggie ID

Root veggies undergo personality changes depending on how you prepare them — did that crisp shredded salad really come from the same vegetable as this creamy, comforting mash? And if the idea of carrots or beetroot in cakes appalls you, just close your eyes and try it anyway!

	Name	Characteristics	Uses
	Carrot	Usually orange, but also purple, yellow or white; usually long and tapering, but also short and stubby or round; firm, juicy texture; sweet flavour	Raw or cooked, in savoury and sweet dishes, salads, soups; cook the short or round ones whole and serve as a side dish to show off their shape
	Parsnip	Ivory flesh; long and tapering; creamy texture, becoming fibrous and woody as they age; distinctive, sweet, nutty flavour	Stews, gratins, soups, mashed, roasted; grate raw young parsnips for salads
	Turnip	Yellowy-orange flesh; fine, fluffy texture; sweet, earthy flavour	Mashed, roasted; grate raw young turnips for salads
	Celeriac	Creamy-white flesh; soft, creamy texture; subtle celery flavour	Mashed, soups, en rémoulade (see below); raw in salads
	Beetroot	Usually purple, but also golden, yellow or ornamental rings; round or cylindrical; firm texture; distinctive, sweet, earthy flavour	Steamed or roasted; cooked or raw in salads; use the leaves as well as the root; loves being partnered with chocolate (see page 91)

TRY IT

Colourful carpaccio A classic carpaccio consists of thin slices of raw meat or fish, but very thinly sliced beetroot makes a gorgeous vegetable alternative — this is where a mandoline is useful, but a Y peeler will do the job if the beetroots are small enough. Try using beetroots in an assortment of colours. Delicious with a herb dressing, goats cheese and toasted pistachio nuts.

127 Veg trinity

The best savoury dishes start with a three-element flavour base so revered by keen cooks that it's called 'the holy trinity'. The elements vary from culture to culture, as does the name given to the trinity — the French call it *mirepoix*, the Italians *soffritto*, the Spanish *sofrito* … The base is often carrot, celery and onion, but one or two elements might be replaced with, for example, garlic, shallot, peppers, fennel or tomato. In Asian cuisine, the trinity is chilli, ginger and garlic, again with variations. Finely chop your trinity of choice and sauté in oil or butter before adding the other ingredients.

126 Rémoulade — a root's best friend

To serve a root vegetable en rémoulade is to shred it and cloak it in mayonnaise dressed up with smooth Dijon mustard, capers and finely chopped cornichons and fresh herbs (parsley, chives, chervil and tarragon). The classic root for rémoulade is celeriac, but it works wonderfully with other roots, either with or without the celeriac — try celeriac and beetroot rémoulade with a hint of grated horseradish. Grate the vegetables (quite coarsely, to give shape and texture) or cut them into thin julienne strips. Toss celeriac in lemon juice to prevent discolouration.

Tuber ID

The edible part of some plants grows underground but is called a tuber in botanical terms rather than a root. The tuber family includes the incredibly versatile potato and the (completely unrelated) sweet potato. Very few veggies fall into the 'tuber' category — these are the most popular.

Name	Characteristics	Uses	Classic dishes	Notes
Potato	Floury or waxy texture; usually white- or cream-fleshed, although there are varieties with purple flesh	Roasting, mashing, baking, French fries, chips, crisps, soups, salads	Tortilla (see page 115); gratin dauphinois; colcannon (see page 84); vichyssoise	Must be eaten cooked; use floury potatoes for methods such as roasting, baking and mashing; waxy potatoes, which hold their shape and texture, for salads
Sweet potato	Variety with bright-orange flesh has moist, creamy texture and sweet, slightly spicy flavour; variety with pale cream flesh resembles a white potato; *Okinawan* variety has deep-purple flesh	Roasting, mashing, baking, soups, curries, salads, baking ingredient	Sweet potato casserole, candied sweet potatoes, sweet potato pudding	Must be eaten cooked; sweet potatoes are often incorrectly called yams (true yams come from a different type of plant)
Jerusalem artichoke (sunchoke)	Knobbly appearance; juicy texture; sweet flavour	Boiling, roasting, mashing, sautéing, soups, salads	Jerusalem artichoke soup	Eat raw or cooked; the high inulin content can cause flatulence in the unwary

128 The ultimate roast potato

The perfect roast potato is crunchy and a little flaky on the outside, fluffy and creamy on the inside and full of flavour.

1 Peel the potatoes and cut them into quite large chunks, because they shrink as they cook. Place them in a pan of cold, salted water, bring to a boil and parboil for about 6–8 minutes. The outsides should be slightly willing to disintegrate.

2 Drain the potatoes in a colander, then shake them well to 'fluff' the outsides. This will create the crisp, crumbly coating.

3 Tip the potatoes into hot fat in a roasting pan. This can be duck or goose fat, olive oil, butter or — if you trust your potato has a really excellent flavour — groundnut oil.

4 Season generously with sea salt and pepper and roast at 190°C (375°F) until golden (about 45 minutes), turning halfway through.

3 Golden rules

129 Roasted potatoes

1 Use the right type of potato — a well-flavoured floury variety, such as Desirée. A waxy potato does not roast successfully — its firm texture and higher water content makes for a leaden centre rather than a light, fluffy one.

2 Let the potatoes dry out for a few minutes in the colander after parboiling and before shaking. Releasing some of the steam makes for a crisper coating and a lighter centre.

3 Make sure the roasting pan is really hot before adding the potatoes, and coat the potatoes in the hot fat, thoroughly but not so vigorously that you undo the fluffing-up.

Choose your flavourings
Flavour your mash with garlic or chopped herbs — or both — to complement the dish you're serving it with.

130 Marvellous mashed potatoes

Mashing potatoes is almost as much of an art as roasting. As with roasted potatoes, use a floury, well-flavoured variety.

1 Cut the potatoes into even-sized chunks and steam (rather than boil) them, with a sprinkling of sea salt, until tender all the way through (this is important — undercooked potatoes mean lumpy mashed potatoes).

2 Remove the steamer basket, cover it with a tea towel to absorb the steam from the potatoes and set aside.

3 Meanwhile, heat some milk in a clean pan (4 tablespoons for four medium potatoes). Add the potatoes and a generous knob of butter, then crush the potatoes with a masher or beat with a heavy fork, until light and fluffy.

131 Are sweet potatoes a good substitute?

Sweet potatoes are delicious, but more characteristic of a root than a tuber, so they're not a 'like-for-like' substitute for white potatoes. They mash and bake, and make a beautiful soup in their own right, whereas too much white potato in a soup makes it unpleasantly gluey. Although sweet potatoes roast well, the result is more like a caramelized root — it's impossible to achieve the crisp, flaky coating and fluffy centre that makes a white roasted potato so appealing.

Tasty greens

Green vegetables hail from the *Brassica* genus (broccoli, cabbage, kale, Brussels sprouts, pak choi), the beetroot family (spinach, chard, beetroot greens) and the legume family (peas, broad beans, green beans).

 132　Keep your greens green

There is nothing less appetizing than a serving of limp, lifeless green vegetables that have completely lost touch with their original vibrant colour. Careful cooking is the answer.

• **Steaming** Make sure the water is boiling before placing the steamer basket on top, then watch carefully, because the moment of perfection passes quickly. Leafy greens wilt as they cook, so you can see when they're done. Test broccoli (the stalk) and green beans for doneness with the tip of a sharp knife. If there's any resistance, cook for a little longer, but keep testing. When the vegetable is cooked, remove the lid and the steamer basket immediately — not only will the water beneath remain hot even when the heat source is turned off, but the veggie will continue cooking in its own residual heat, and what looked and tasted fresh and appetizing will rapidly be overdone.

• **Boiling/blanching** Bring salted water to a boil before adding the vegetables and cook until just tender. Drain immediately.

• **Wilting** Tender leafy greens can be wilted in just the water clinging to the leaves after rinsing. Place the leaves (sliced if necessary) in a pan, sprinkle with salt and cook over a medium heat, stirring occasionally to prevent sticking and burning, until just wilted. Drain the leaves thoroughly as soon as they're cooked — they give off a surprising amount of water.

Once the greens are cooked, rinse them under cold running water or, better still, plunge them into iced water. This arrests the cooking and preserves the colour. Reheat very quickly in a little butter or olive oil to serve as a side dish or add at the last minute to other ingredients.

Save the spinach
Tender greens such as spinach all but disappear very quickly when cooked, so always overestimate how much to use.

TRY IT

A taste of the Irish Colcannon is an Irish dish that combines mashed potato with shredded kale or green cabbage. It's a delicious accompaniment to most things, but especially to boiled or baked ham. Mash the potatoes (see page 83), then either lightly steam the kale or cabbage or sauté with thinly sliced leeks in butter or bacon fat, until just wilted. Stir into the potatoes. The traditional way to serve colcannon is in a mountain on the plate, with a volcanic crater full of melting butter into which you dip forkfuls of potato. Alternatively, add extra butter to the mashed potatoes.

5 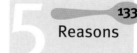 **133 Reasons to keep a bag of petits pois in your freezer**

1 Thaw a handful and add to more or less anything—risotto, curry, pasta—at the last minute for instant colour and texture.

2 Warm the peas in a base of shallots and pancetta sautéed in butter and vegetable stock, then blend to make a pale green soup.

3 Sauté leeks and little gem lettuce, then stir in petits pois and a little water and braise gently to make a French-inspired side dish for chicken or, with chopped mint, for lamb.

4 Make a minted pea purée and swipe a spoonful flamboyantly on a white plate to accompany scallops or prawns.

5 Blend with yoghurt, mint, lemon zest and juice, and grated hard, salty cheese such as Parmesan to make a refreshing dip.

Go wild ID

Bored with broccoli or just plain broke? Then forage for your greens — with expert guidance, if you're inexperienced. Here are five of the best:

Name	Characteristics	Season	Where?	Ways to use
Fiddleheads	Bright green, succulent, unfurled tips of the ostrich (or shuttlecock) fern; fresh, grassy flavour with hints of asparagus and spinach	Very short season — 2–3 weeks in spring	Found in the wild in Europe, North America and Asia; available from specialist suppliers in the UK	Remove brown scales, rinse thoroughly and use immediately; do not eat raw. Sauté in butter; steam and use in tarts or pasta dishes or serve with hollandaise sauce; deep-fry in tempura batter
Nettles	Bright green, tender young tips; fresh, earthy flavour. Easy to identify — edible nettles are the ones that sting when raw (ouch!), so wear rubber gloves to pick and prepare	Best in spring, but cut nettles continue to throw up new young shoots throughout summer	Abundant in Europe, North America, Asia and Africa	Wilt nettles in boiling water to remove the sting. Use wherever you'd use spinach — in soup, as a ravioli filling, in pesto or risotto, steamed as a side dish
Dandelion	Long, slender, jagged leaves; tangy, bitter flavour, similar to endive, chicory and rocket. Easy to identify — look for the sunny yellow (edible) flowers followed by the distinctive seed head	Best in spring, when the young leaves are at their least bitter; later in the year, blanch for 3–5 minutes to reduce bitterness	Abundant worldwide	Sauté with sweet onion or pancetta to balance the bitterness; eat very young leaves raw in salad; toss boiled older leaves with butter
Sorrel	Fresh green shield- or clover-shaped leaves; tangy, sour, lemony flavour; high in oxalic acid (so should be avoided by those with kidney problems)	Spring and summer	Abundant in parts of Europe and North America; also cultivated	Combine with other ingredients to balance sourness; eat young leaves raw, dressed with olive oil; older leaves in soup, pesto, sauce to accompany oily fish
Samphire	Succulent, salty, slender, crunchy, fresh green branched stalks; also known as sea beans, sea asparagus, glasswort	Spring and summer	Abundant in coastal areas and salt marshes in North America, Europe, South Africa and South Asia	Raw or blanched in salad; lightly steamed and tossed in butter to accompany fish or salt-marsh lamb; pesto. No need to add salt!

134 Snap!

A newly harvested asparagus stalk immediately starts to become woody and fibrous, a process called lignification — so unless you have extremely fresh asparagus, you need to remove the tough end (the bit that was in the ground) before cooking. Hold the stalk between the forefinger and thumb of both hands at the point where it turns from white to green, and snap it. The woody end should break off naturally — but if it doesn't, move your fingers up a little and try again. Use the woody ends in soup or homemade vegetable stock — they might be unappealing to eat, but they still have lots of flavour.

135 Flavoursome stock

A well-flavoured vegetable stock is as important to get right as a meat or fish stock. The 'holy trinity' vegetables (see page 81) provide a good base — onions (or leek), carrots and celery. A good balance is one large onion, two large carrots and four celery stalks, with additional flavourings (see Three Golden Rules). Beyond that, much depends on how you'll be using the stock. Tomato pulp adds flavour but also colour; beetroot is a no-no unless you want pink stock. Cruciferous vegetables such as cabbage and cauliflower can be overpowering, as can asparagus, so add these in small quantities, if at all. Chop the vegetables roughly, cover them with water in a pan, bring the water almost to a boil, simmer gently for 1 hour, then strain.

TRY IT

Echalion shallots If the trickiness of peeling a traditional round shallot frustrates you, use echalion shallots instead — they're far easier to peel and chop. Dubbed 'banana' shallots because of their tapered oval shape, this type is a cross between an onion and shallot, with an excellent flavour.

3 Golden rules   **137** ## Sumptuous stock

1 Scrub vegetables thoroughly before peeling so that you can save the peelings for the stockpot. Discard the tops of carrots, unless they are organic — carrot-fly pesticide collects in the 'shoulders'.

2 If you need a clear stock for your recipe, avoid potatoes and their peelings. They will release starch and 'cloud' the stock.

3 Add depth to the flavour with fennel bulb, mushroom stalks, bay leaves, parsley stalks, sprigs of thyme, peppercorns and, if you like, garlic cloves and strips of thinly pared lemon zest.

5 Reasons   **136** **to keep some spinach nuggets in your freezer**

1 Add a handful to a rustic vegetable soup or stew at the end of cooking.

2 Stir into a risotto for colour and texture.

3 Stir into ricotta cheese with freshly grated nutmeg to make a filling for ravioli.

4 Thaw a few nuggets, pat dry with kitchen paper and scatter on top of a homemade pizza.

5 Heat through a generous quantity in a drizzle of olive oil and mix in a blender with strained yoghurt, a squeeze of lemon juice, a grating of nutmeg and a handful of freshly grated Parmesan or Pecorino to make a quick sauce for pasta. Remember to save some pasta water to finish the sauce.

Sauce in seconds
When blending sauces that contain cooked-from-frozen spinach, use the pulse button to make sure you retain some texture.

Mushrooms: A classic addition

Useful for adding flavour, texture and visual appeal to all sorts of savoury dishes, cultivated fresh mushrooms are available year-round in an increasingly adventurous range of varieties.

 138 Give them space

A mushroom is mostly water so if you crowd them together in a frying pan, they'll steam rather than brown and shrink rapidly. Sauté them in batches if necessary, in a single layer and with space around them, over a medium-high heat — it's very important to have the frying pan hot enough to sear them as they hit the pan. Chestnut mushrooms have a lower water content than the smaller, white ones, so are firmer and retain their shape and texture better.

139 Mushroom duxelles — why bother?

Mushroom duxelles is nothing more sophisticated than finely chopped mushrooms, onions and shallots sautéed in butter — but it punches way above its weight in umami. Melt a generous knob of unsalted butter in a frying pan and add the prepared vegetables (one onion and one large shallot to 250 g /9 oz finely chopped mushrooms). Season to taste and cook over medium-high heat until the liquid has evaporated, leaving a thick purée full of concentrated flavour.

• Stir a spoonful into any savoury dish to add colour and intensify the flavour.
• Add chopped fresh tarragon or sage and use to fill ravioli.
• Stir in wilted spinach, a hint of double cream and a sprinkle of freshly grated nutmeg to serve as a side dish.
• Wrap a piece of beef fillet in a pancake, slather with mushroom duxelles and encase in puff pastry for a beef Wellington.

TRY IT

Truffle salt Truffles (the fungus, not the chocolate imitation) have acquired the status of a precious commodity, and are beyond the price range of the average cook. However, truffle salt is more manageable and adds a hint of the real thing to risotto, pasta, scrambled eggs — whatever you like. Share a jar with a friend and halve the cost!

TRY IT

Mushroom brush The easiest way to remove the specks of compost that tend to cling to commercially grown mushrooms is with a soft, dry mushroom brush (choose one shaped like a mushroom to remind you of its sole purpose). Soaking fresh mushrooms tends to make them slimy. It's fine, however, to rinse off persistent compost or soil if you dry the mushrooms immediately with kitchen paper.

Crusty crostini
Mushroom duxelles is an ideal topping for crostini — the toast soaks up all the buttery mushroom flavour.

Mushroom ID

Mushrooms range from cultivated and inexpensive to wild and highly prized. Even the cheapest have plenty to offer in terms of taste, texture and usefulness.

	Name	Characteristics	Uses ...
	Button	White, closed cap; firm texture; mild flavour	The all-purpose everyday mushroom
	Chestnut	Brown, closed cap; firm, meaty texture; rich, earthy flavour	Good with hearty meat and vegetable dishes
	Portobello (large), portabellini (small)	Brown, flat, open cap; firm, meaty texture; rich, earthy flavour	Perfect for stuffing (use the stalk in the filling or to flavour stocks, etc.)
	Shiitake	Brown, open cap with hard stem (remove before cooking the cap and use to flavour stocks); firm, meaty texture; rich, meaty flavour, intensifies when dried	Good in Asian dishes
	Maitake	Fan-shaped, ruffled-feather appearance, grows in clusters; firm texture; rich, earthy flavour	Good in Asian dishes with noodles, or with risotto to show off appearance
	Oyster	Oyster colour and shape; fragile, melting texture; sweet, subtle flavour	Good in Asian dishes; mix with more robust mushrooms for texture
	Morel	Conical, honeycomb cap; only grows in the wild; often dried; spongy texure; smoky, nutty, earthy flavour; toxic when raw	Sauté in butter; good with eggs or steak, pasta or risotto
	Enoki	Tiny button cap on long stem; crunchy texture; mild flavour	Raw in salads or cooked in Asian-style broth
	Porcini	Brown cap on sturdy white stalk; meaty texture; strong, earthy flavour; readily available dried	Add to meaty casseroles or to risotto or pasta dishes

Warning: Foraging can be dangerous to your health

Foraged mushrooms are wonderful, but only when you're foraging with an expert, or are an expert yourself. **The potential for picking a poisonous specimen is too great otherwise.**

Vegetable fruits

Some plant foods used in a savoury or 'vegetable' context are, strictly speaking, fruits — tomatoes, cucumber, aubergine, peppers and chillies, avocados and the squashes, including courgettes, are all fruits.

140   Easy peeling

The peel or skin of most vegetable fruits is edible. However, some recipes require the skin to be removed. It's possible to peel some of the vegetable fruits with a Y peeler, whereas others need a more devious technique.

Cucumber, courgette The easiest to peel, if indeed you want to bother. Strip off the peel lengthways with a Y peeler.

Other squash Use a Y peeler for butternut squash, but you might need to go over the same area more than once. Alternatively (and for pumpkin), cut away the skin using a sharp knife — or simply roast the squash with the peel on. Once roasted, the flesh comes away easily and has a fabulous flavour.

Tomato Make a shallow, cross-shape incision in the top and base of the tomato. Dip it into boiling water and be ready to remove it as soon as the skin starts to peel back at the incisions. Plunge the tomato into a bowl of cold water for 5 minutes, then peel.

Aubergine, peppers, chillies Cook with the stalk intact over an open gas flame, on a grill or griddle pan or in a hot oven, turning occasionally, until the skin starts to blacken and blister. Place in a freezer bag, seal the top and let cool for 10 minutes. Holding the vegetable fruit by its stalk, peel off the skin.

Avocado Tackle this one from the inside out. Cut the avocado in half lengthways, then either slice or dice the flesh and turn the skin inside out to release it, or scoop out the flesh with a spoon.

141   Less water, more flavour

Roasting tomatoes in a cool oven drives off excess water and really intensifies the flavour. Halve the tomatoes and toss them gently in olive oil and black pepper. Place on a roasting tray and roast at 140°C (275°F) for 1½ hours. Add a few garlic cloves or sprigs of thyme if you like. Try the same technique with young courgette, cut into quarters lengthways — but, before roasting, sprinkle the quarters with sea salt flakes and set aside for a half hour to draw off some of the water. Rinse and dry thoroughly with kitchen paper before tossing in the olive oil.

FIX IT

Removing the stone from a tenacious avocado Cut the avocado in half lengthways around the stone (1) and twist the two halves to separate them (2). Cup the half with the stone lightly in one hand, then give the stone a sharp rap (widthways, to avoid your fingers) with the blade of a heavy kitchen knife. Twist the knife and the stone will meekly part from the avocado (3).

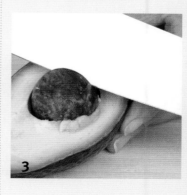

142   The versatile avocado

Avocado is perhaps the only plant food that sits completely comfortably in both the savoury and sweet camps. It's great in salads, a classic pairing with prawns and the star attraction in dips such as guacamole; but it's also stunning in smoothies, ice cream and chocolate mousse.

Avocado dip Mash together (or blend, for a smooth dip) a ripe avocado with 2 tablespoons of soured cream or strained yoghurt, 1 tablespoon of coconut oil, 1 teaspoon of finely grated lemon or lime zest, a crushed garlic clove, a sprinkling of chilli flakes and a few fresh mint leaves, finely chopped. Season with salt and pepper.

Avocado mousse Soak three chopped fresh dates (ideally Medjool) in 1 tablespoon of water, then blend with a ripe avocado, 1 teaspoon of vanilla extract, 1 tablespoon of unsweetened cocoa powder and a pinch of salt. Add honey to taste if you have a very sweet tooth.

VEGGIE CAKE FLAVOUR COMBOS

Once you accept that carrots aren't the only vegetable that tastes good in cakes, the creative sky is the limit. Try the following combinations:

Beetroot   chocolate   cardamom

Courgette   hazelnuts   cinnamon

Sweet potato   orange   ginger

143   Chillies without tears

Chillies contain the irritant capsaicin, and need to be handled with care. To avoid inflicting burning pain on yourself, chop the chilli without handling it.

1 Anchor the chilli at the stalk end with a fork and slice it lengthways. Trim off the stalk.

2 Still using the fork as an anchor, use a teaspoon to scrape away the seeds and white membrane from each half (scrape them up with the kitchen knife and dispose of them without touching).

3 Slice each half of the chilli into thin strips lengthways, leaving the stalk end intact.

4 Chop the chilli into fine dice.

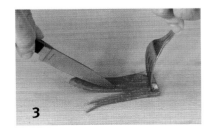

Juicy fruit

Fruit — citrus in particular — adds all sorts of good things to cooking: sharpness to cut through rich ingredients, sweetness to balance sour, bitter and salty flavours, as well as texture and a satisfying juiciness.

 ### 144 Marinating — the principles

A marinade has two purposes — to tenderize and to flavour. Acidic ingredients such as citrus fruits take care of the tenderizing process, whereas flavour is added in the form of oil and herbs/spices (use equal quantities of oil and the acidic ingredient). The choice of ingredients can take the same cut of meat on a global culinary journey.

Take a chicken breast, for example, and try one of the following marinades:

• **Asian flavour** Groundnut oil, lime juice, coriander, garlic, chilli and ginger

• **Mediterranean twist** Olive oil, lemon juice, thyme, oregano and garlic

• **Moroccan magic** Argan oil, orange juice, cumin seed, caraway seed, crushed red pepper

 ### 145 Watch the clock!

It's important not to over-marinate in an acidic ingredient. For example, a delicate ingredient such as fish will start to 'cook' very quickly — it's the principle of dishes such as ceviche, where marinating fish in lime or other citrus juice for just 10 minutes denatures the protein in the same way that cooking does. Certain non-citrus fruits contain enzymes that do almost too good a job in a marinade — the bromelain in pineapple and papain in papaya are highly effective enzymes that would devour meat if left too long, whereas kiwi fruit contains actinidin, a less aggressive enzyme.

146 Lemon alternative

Need lemon freshness but have no lemons? Keep a jar of sumac in your spice rack for just such an occasion. It's a Middle Eastern spice with the tartness of lemon and can be used in marinades, dressings and risottos, and to flavour olive oil, fish, meat and vegetables. For marinades and dressings, you can use white wine vinegar instead of lemon juice — 3 tablespoons of vinegar is roughly equivalent to the juice of one lemon.

3 Golden rules

147 Marinating meat

1 Marinate in a china or glass dish, but never metal (the acidity in the marinade might react with the metal). Smaller cuts and individual portions can be marinated in a robust freezer bag with a slide seal.

2 Always marinate the meat in the refrigerator to avoid bacterial growth — chicken and other poultry for a maximum of two days, and all other types of meat for a maximum of five days.

3 Turn the meat in the marinade occasionally if it's not completely immersed. A sealed freezer bag makes this very easy — just massage the meat through the bag.

Prawns love lemon
Try using freshly grated lemon zest as a garnish — it looks pretty against the orange-pink colour of prawns, for example.

TRY IT

Separate zest from pith To pare the thin layer of lemon zest efficiently from the bitter white pith, either pare off strips with a Y peeler, scrape off strands with a lemon zester (see below) or grate it with a fine grater, such as a Microplane.

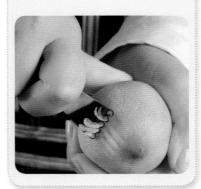

148 Wax on, wax off

Unless you specifically hunt out untreated citrus fruit, it will have been coated in wax to prolong its shelf life. Before using the zest, scrub the fruit in hot water and washing up liquid, then rinse well in hot water and dry with kitchen paper. But if you have a choice, take the unwaxed option.

5 Reasons

149 to keep a couple of lemons in your fridge

1 Just a squeeze of lemon balances sweet flavours in certain foods such as butternut squash and sweet potatoes.

2 Two drops of lemon juice added to egg whites before whisking stabilizes the foam and adds volume.

3 Use lemon juice to sour milk for soda bread (see page 139).

4 An oil and lemon dressing is excellent for a salad containing sweet fruits — the lemon serves the double purpose of balancing the sweetness and preventing the fruit from turning brown through oxidation.

5 Grated lemon zest makes just about everything zing, from salads to cakes and biscuits. If it feels right, add some!

Dried fruit tagine

The rich, sweet flavour and slightly chewy texture of dried fruit marries well with meat, and the combination appears in many culinary traditions. Prunes are particularly good with wild game, such as rabbit, venison and wild boar, but go equally well with beef and pork; apricots, which are slightly sharper, with lamb and chicken. A Moroccan tagine is a great way to experiment.

Ingredients
1 unwaxed orange, washed and dried
150 g (5 oz) dried apricots
2 tbsp olive oil
1 large onion, finely sliced
1.25 kg (2¾ lb) shoulder of lamb, cubed
½ tsp ground cumin
¼ tsp cinnamon
Salt and pepper
1 tbsp ground almonds
300 ml water
Toasted almonds, to garnish

1 Finely grate the orange zest and set aside, then squeeze the juice into a bowl. Add the apricots and set aside to plump up.
2 Heat the oil in the base of a flameproof tagine or a casserole dish over a medium heat, add the onion and cook for about 10 minutes, stirring occasionally, until soft and golden brown.
3 Add the meat, cumin and cinnamon, season to taste with salt and pepper and stir well for 5 minutes.
4 Add the orange juice with the apricots, orange zest, almonds and water.
5 Cover and bring to a simmer. When the liquid is bubbling, reduce the heat to medium-low and continue to cook, stirring occasionally, for about 40 minutes, or until the lamb is cooked. Serve with couscous (see page 71) and garnish with toasted almonds.

150 Jelly: The perfect companion

One of the most satisfying accompaniments to meat and game (and warm toast) is a clear, tart yet sweet, jewel-coloured fruit jelly. Ripe berries are perfect (cranberries, blackberries, sloes, red currants) and sharp apples, crab apples, green guavas and quinces are wonderful, too, either on their own or as a source of pectin to help set a berry jam or jelly. A few unripe berries also help the set. Make as little or as much jelly as you want — it keeps really well.

1 Prepare the fruit, discarding any that is damaged. Rinse well, then place in a heavy pan, add cold water to three-quarters the depth of the fruit and simmer until soft.
2 Suspend a jelly bag (or improvise with muslin) above a bowl, tip in the fruit and let it stand overnight for the juice to drip into the bowl. Resist the temptation to force it through with a spoon — this might cloud the jelly.
3 Measure the juice and place in a pan with sugar — as a rule of thumb, 450 g (1 lb) sugar to 600 ml juice. Bring to the boil and boil until the jelly reaches setting point.
4 Drop a teaspoonful onto a cold plate to test if it's set. Decant into small, warm, sterilized jars and seal with waxed paper.

Juicy jelly
Dark-coloured fruits, such as blackberries, damsons or sloes, make a rich jelly with plenty of depth.

151 Fruit and fish? Really?

A sauce or purée made from a tart fruit — the sort that makes you wince if you eat it unsweetened — is the perfect complement for oily fish, the acidity of the fruit balancing the richness of the fish. Try mackerel with rhubarb, trout with gooseberries or salmon with red or black currants.

Salad of contrasts
Try a really simple salad of flaked, salty mackerel with a sharp green apple, chopped into pieces, topped with ginger and lime dressing.

FRUIT IN SALAD FLAVOUR COMBOS

The combination of sweet, juicy fruit with crisp salad greens, salty cheese and a sharp lemon and olive oil dressing satisfies every single taste bud in one appetizing hit. For a rustic, eat-me look, tear the fruit into pieces and crumble soft cheese, rather than slicing it all neatly. Try the following combinations:

Pear + watercress + blue cheese

Nectarine + rocket + Parmesan shavings

Fig + spinach + feta

Herbal magic

The range of plants classified as herbs is vast. Some have substantial leaves and are used as a vegetable in their own right, for eating raw or lightly steamed, whereas others are used in smaller or even tiny quantities for their powerful flavour.

 152 Is it a herb? Is it a spice?

A herb is a plant used in cooking for its aromatic leaves. A spice (see pages 100–101) is the fruit of a plant — the berry or seed destined to become a new plant. In some cases, such as dill and herb fennel, both the leaves and the fruit of a plant are used (the fruit is more intensely flavoured than the herb). Some herbs and spices are only used in savoury cooking — parsley and cumin, for example, are never likely to catch on in desserts — but many translate readily into both savoury and sweet dishes.

153 Herbs that dry beautifully (and ones that really don't)

Herbs were dried traditionally because there was no other option for preserving them. But they're not all suited to drying.
• **'Woody'-stemmed herbs** — sage, rosemary, bay, thyme and mint family (mint, marjoram, oregano) — dry well, and in some cultures the dried herb is used in preference to fresh.
• **Soft herbs**, such as parsley, basil, tarragon, coriander and chives, lose all their freshness when dried and are better frozen. Commercially, the two methods are combined in freeze-drying, which preserves the flavour and aroma of the herb — well worth seeking out if you don't grow your own.

Pestle perfection
Choose a really robust pestle to make short work of grinding even the most resistant spices.

TRY IT

Herb chopper A *mezzaluna* ('half moon') or hachoir is the traditional tool for chopping herbs. The curved blade with double handles enables you to rock it over the herbs, changing direction as necessary. It often comes with a board with a concave surface, giving you even better control.

 154 Pestle and mortar

The pestle and mortar combo is an unsung hero of kitchen equipment and often a thing of beauty. The mortar is the bowl and the pestle the club-shaped tool, although some modern pestles are shaped more like knobs — either way, the important element is the rounded surface that engages with the mortar. It's used for pounding (herbs, garlic, ginger, pastes, dips) and grinding (spices, sea salt, nuts, seeds). A huge advantage is that it handles tiny quantities — if you only want a pinch of spice, that's all you need grind.

Herb ID

This is a selection of the most useful fresh herbs to use in cooking, and the ones to grow in your herb garden. Some will even grow in a pot on the windowsill.

Name	Characteristics	Good with ...	Notes
Parsley	Robust flat or curly leaves; strong, distinctive, appetizing aroma and flavour	Salads, especially tabbouleh; marinades, stocks, soups, sauces; add to butter for glazing vegetables	The most versatile herb; flat-leaf considered to have the better flavour; ingredient in bouquet garni and *fines herbes*
Rosemary	Sharp, spiky, strongly aromatic leaves; pungent flavour	Meat, fish, vegetables, marinades; use sparingly in desserts and baking	Add whole sprig for flavouring and remove before serving; otherwise strip off leaves and chop finely
Thyme	Tiny, soft, aromatic leaves; intense, pungent flavour	Meat, fish, vegetables, stuffings; wonderful ingredient in baking	Strip off the leaves and discard the stems; ingredient in bouquet garni
Sage	Soft, strongly aromatic, green-grey leaves; slightly bitter flavour	Meat, vegetables, pasta, gnocchi; sizzle in butter as a garnish	Use sparingly as flavour can be overpowering
Oregano/ marjoram	Closely related herbs; small aromatic leaves; pungent flavour	Mediterranean dishes; vegetables, tomatoes, meat, legumes; oregano good with lamb	Strip off the leaves and discard the stems
Bay	Robust, shiny, aromatic leaves; pungent, bittersweet flavour	Marinades, meat dishes, tomato sauce; add to pan when cooking legumes; infuse in milk for white sauce; rice pudding	Ingredient in bouquet garni; aroma and flavour improve when dried; discard after cooking
Coriander	Leaves similar to flat-leaf parsley; distinctive, love-it-or-hate-it aroma and taste	Asian and Central/South American cuisine, avocados, e.g., guacamole	Fresh leaves are best eaten very young, before the flavour becomes overpowering; works well with hot chillies
Basil	Tender, aromatic leaf, varies in size and flavour depending on variety	Tomatoes, salads, vegetables; key ingredient in pesto Genovese (sweet basil); Thai curries (tulsi/holy basil)	Loses its aroma and flavour when dried
Chives	Narrow, hollow leaves; mild onion flavour	Eggs, salads	Ingredient in fines herbes
Dill	Fine, feathery leaves; celery/aniseed flavour	Fish (especially in gravlax), soured cream, potato salad, vegetables	Use to flavour gherkins and white wine or apple cider vinegar
Chervil	Delicate leaves; mild, slightly sweet aniseed flavour	White fish, eggs, sauces, soups, salads, vegetables	Ingredient in fines herbes
Tarragon	Narrow, pointed leaves; aniseed flavour	Chicken, fish, sauces	Ingredient in fines herbes; French tarragon has a more delicate flavour than Russian
Mint	Robust, broad or long leaves; fresh aroma and flavour	Lamb, duck, vegetables, tabbouleh, legumes, yoghurt dips, sauces; ice cream	Mint comes in many variations

1 Assemble the aromatics — the ones shown here (bay leaves, fennel, marjoram, parsley) help make a tasty stock for fish.

2 Wrap a length of lemon zest around the herbs to hold them together and add flavour. Cut off as much of the white pith as possible.

3 Tie the bouquet garni firmly with string — if the bundle falls apart in the pot, you'll be picking stalks out later on.

4 Ready to go! Your beautiful bundle will be a soggy mess at the end of cooking, but the food will taste great.

155   Heavenly bundle of flavour

A bouquet garni is a selection of fresh aromatic herbs tied into a bunch and used to flavour stews, stock, sauces, soups — the advantage being that at the end of cooking, you lift out the bundle, leaving no evidence but the flavour. Simply tie the herbs together with unwaxed kitchen twine, or attach them to a stick of celery or a leek leaf; alternatively, tie them into a square of muslin (use this method for dried herbs, too).

- **Classic French** Parsley, thyme, bay leaf

- **Italian** Rosemary, thyme, bay leaf

- **For fish** (shown left) Parsley, lemon thyme, bay leaf, marjoram, fennel stalk, lemon zest

- **For beef** Parsley, thyme, bay leaf, marjoram, orange zest

- **For pork** Parsley, thyme, bay leaf, marjoram, juniper

- **For chicken** Tarragon, chervil, salad burnet, lemon zest

Beware of beauty
If in doubt about whether a flower is edible, don't risk it. Some of the prettiest flowers are highly poisonous. However, the pretty ones that are edible make a very colourful addition to a risotto.

156   Fines herbes

Jazz up an omelette with this classic mix of fresh herbs. Combine 2 tablespoons each of chopped parsley and chervil with 1 tablespoon of chopped chives and a few chopped French tarragon leaves.

157   Eat the flowers!

Many herbs have really pretty — and edible — flowers that look gorgeous scattered over a salad and add a delicate flavour, a more subtle version of the leaf. Borage, viola, chives, calendula (marigold), nasturtium, mint, sage, dandelion, daisy and violet are just a few.

Essential garlic

One of the oldest cultivated plants in the world, garlic is the most pungent member of its family, which includes leeks, chives and spring onions. If you hate the aftertaste, just chew on some parsley!

158 Useful tool or culinary no-no?

It's easy enough to mince garlic — either chop it quite finely, add a pinch of salt and press it with the flat of a kitchen knife, scraping it together and pressing again until crushed to a smooth paste, or crush it with a pinch of salt using a pestle and mortar. Alternatively, a traditional garlic press or the latest innovation, a 'rocker' crusher, does the job less messily. Using a tool to crush garlic is controversial, however — some chefs look upon presses with disdain, claiming the process creates a harsh flavour. And garlic crushers are wasteful — some of the clove inevitably stays in the press.

Vivid greenery
Stir gremolata into cooked dishes just before serving to preserve the colour of the parsley, which can be finely or roughly chopped as preferred.

159 Peeling cloves

Peeling a garlic clove can be frustrating — the skin is papery and the clove slightly tacky. The trick is to trim off the base of the clove, then lay a kitchen knife flat on the clove and press firmly with the heel of your hand. The clove flattens and separates, loosening the skin.

160 Mellower tones

Roasting garlic mellows out the flavour. 'Wet' garlic is perfect for roasting, or use a dried bulb with plump cloves and no sign of shooting. Slice off the top of the bulb so the clove flesh is visible, sprinkle with salt and thyme leaves, drizzle with olive oil or dot with butter, and roast at 170°C (325°F) for about 30 minutes, or until the flesh is soft and yielding. You can also add individual cloves, unpeeled, when you're roasting roots, and squish out the flesh when they're soft.

161 Gorgeous gremolata

Gremolata is a quick and easy taste boost made from four of the simplest and best flavours in cooking — parsley, garlic, lemon zest and black pepper. Finely chop a large handful of fresh flat-leaf parsley and mix with two crushed fat garlic cloves (or roasted, see above) and the finely grated zest of a lemon. Season with black pepper. It's very good with fish, chicken and virtually everything.

Variety of spice

Spices provide the element of 'je ne sais quoi' in a dish — warming, pungent, often visibly indiscernible but definitely there.

162 Peppercorns: The king of spice

Pepper is derived from the dried berry fruit of a tropical vine. Nothing says 'dinner's ready' more eloquently than the last twist of the pepper mill before you tuck in — but there's more to it than freshly ground black pepper.

Black Salt's natural friend, and the one that is meant when 'season to taste with salt and pepper' is specified. Black peppercorns have a rich, warm flavour.

White The peppercorn to choose for 'pale' dishes such as white sauces, creamy soups, even mashed potatoes if you prefer not to see black flecks. White pepper is hotter than black.

Green This one is robust and bold and really holds its own against rich meat.

Pink These pretty pseudo peppercorns have a sweet, slightly astringent flavour. Unlike true peppercorns, they're light and hollow and need to be crushed rather than ground. They work well in both savoury and sweet dishes.

163 Substitutes — dare you?

The idea of using one herb or spice when the recipe clearly states another sounds reckless, but some are quite comparable in flavour despite coming from a different plant family. For example, several spice seeds have an aniseed flavour (anise, star anise, fennel, caraway, dill), as do the herbs chervil, dill, French tarragon and sweet basil. So if you need to use a substitute, you can often get away with it — as long as it has a similar taste profile.

164 Salt: Pepper's friend

Neither a herb nor a spice, but an essential seasoning and the natural companion to pepper. Salt is a touchy subject — but if you only ever eat home-cooked, unprocessed food, you'll be in complete control of your salt intake. Lecture over! The purpose of salt is not to make bland food palatable, but to enhance the natural flavour of good food, both savoury and sweet. Invest in a good-quality, unrefined sea salt such as Atlantic, Celtic or the delightfully named fleur de sel ('flower of salt'), and you'll only need a pinch. Flavoured sea salts, available from artisan food shops, are really useful — they're pricey but pack a huge punch and save time.

165 Dedicated grinder

It's very difficult to grind spices to a fine powder, even with a pestle and mortar, so if you use them fairly often, it's worth getting a spice grinder — essentially a coffee grinder with a different name, either manual or electric. Whole spices freshly ground have a far superior flavour to those you buy ready ground.

Spice ID

These are some of the most versatile spices, used in a number of cuisines worldwide. Note that some spices have variations with completely different flavour profiles and are not interchangeable.

Name	Characteristics	Good with ...	Notes
Cumin	Small, crescent-shaped seeds with a strong, pungent aroma and earthy, smoky flavour	Indian and Middle Eastern cuisine; meat, fish, vegetables	Nigella seed is sometimes called 'black' cumin seed but has a completely different flavour to white cumin so is not a substitute
Coriander	Aromatic seeds with a sweet citrus flavour	Meat, fish, vegetables; baking and desserts	Coriander is a component of several classic spice blends, such as harissa (see page 103)
Cardamom	Small green pods with an enticing aroma and warm, sweet flavour	Indian, Middle Eastern and Scandinavian cuisine; meat, fish, vegetables; desserts and baking (loves chocolate)	Use lightly crushed whole pods or extract the seeds; black cardamom has a smoky aroma and flavour so is not a substitute for green
Fennel	Small green seeds with a warm, sweet aroma and aniseed flavour	Meat, fish, vegetables, legumes; baking	Fennel pollen ('the spice of angels') is even sweeter and more intense than the seeds — very expensive but a little goes a long way
Chilli	Small hot peppers in a variety of shapes, sizes and colours; available fresh, dried, as flakes or ground	Meat, fish, vegetables; desserts and baking (loves chocolate)	Fresh chillies can really make their presence felt, so always use the variety specified in the recipe
Paprika	Bright red powder made from dried and ground hot, sweet peppers	European and Mexican cuisine; meat, fish, vegetables, eggs	Smoked paprika is a rich, deep red with a distinctive sweet, smoky flavour
Star anise	Star-shaped spice with a strong, sweet licorice/anise aroma and flavour	Chinese cuisine, especially duck and pork; vegetables; desserts, mulled wine	Star anise is the key ingredient in Chinese five-spice powder
Cloves	Dried flower buds with a sweet, spicy aroma and flavour	Meat, vegetables, fresh and dried fruit; baking and desserts, mulled wine	Cloves are the perfect design for spiking — into onions, ham, oranges, etc.
Cinnamon	Aromatic dried bark rolled into quills, with a warm, sweet flavour	Meat, marinades, vegetables, fresh and dried fruit; baking and desserts (loves chocolate), mulled wine	Quills are hard to grind; use whole or broken and remove before serving
Nutmeg	Gnarled nut-shaped fruit of the nutmeg tree; warm, spicy aroma and flavour	Béchamel sauce, root and green vegetables; baking and desserts	Freshly grate whole nutmeg as required; use sparingly to avoid overpowering
Vanilla	Long dark brown pod full of tiny, fragrant seeds with a sweet flavour; also available as powder, paste, or extract for baking	Traditionally used in baking and to flavour custards and custard-based dishes such as ice cream; daring cooks use it in sides to accompany meat and fish dishes	Place 'spent' vanilla pods in a jar with caster sugar to use in baking

 166 Ginger it up

Ginger — pale, knobbly, uninspiring in appearance — is a magic ingredient. So good, in fact, that it's used as a verb — 'to ginger something up' means to make it more exciting. A must in many Asian dishes, ginger also adds a zing to dips, vegetables (try it with spinach), desserts and more. It softens but tends to hold its shape when cooked, so if you don't want the texture, either grate it, crush it using a pestle and mortar or chop it really finely. Ground ginger powder is more fiery but can be used as a substitute for fresh if it's your only choice; however, this doesn't work well in reverse, for example in baking.

167 Left on the shelf

What do you do with the spices you bought for one dish and never used again? The answer is — be creative. Spices do wonderful and unexpected things for vegetables, grains, baking and desserts.

- **Nutmeg** Spinach, cabbage (green or red), mushrooms
- **Cumin** Root vegetables, couscous, quinoa
- **Caraway seeds** Root vegetables, red cabbage, cakes, biscuits
- **Fennel seeds** Sourdough bread, cheese biscuits
- **Green cardamom** Crème brûlée, cakes

168 Sophisticated saffron

The bright orange stigmas of the crocus that yields this spice are picked by hand, so it's expensive, but a little goes a long way. Saffron has a woody, floral aroma and a subtle bittersweet flavour. Use it to colour rice dishes such as risotto, paella and pilaf, in fish stews and in baking. Infuse the 'threads' in warm water, then add to the dish to colour and flavour it. Turmeric is used as a substitute to colour rice, but it's no substitute for the flavour.

169 Caper addict

The flower buds of a Mediterranean shrub, capers have a distinctive sour flavour — an acquired taste but, once acquired, it's rather addictive. The tiny variety considered to have the best flavour are known as *nonpareille* ('unrivaled'). Capers are preserved in brine, vinegar, oil or dry salt. They go well with Mediterranean vegetables and herbs, and with meat, fish, pasta sauces and pizza.

170 Chinese five-spice

This is a lovely blend of warm, fragrant star anise and cinnamon with cloves, fennel seed and Sichuan pepper (possibly also ginger and nutmeg, but it's still called five-spice). Use it in marinades and rubs for meat and in stir-fries and rice dishes. And biscuits!

North African harissa

A gorgeous colour and enticingly aromatic, it's easy to make your own simple version of harissa paste. Store a batch in the refrigerator (covering the surface with a thin layer of olive oil) and use as a marinade, to spice up couscous, pasta sauces or soup, as a drizzle for roasted roots (see pages 80–81) or even just for dunking sourdough bread (see page 139). Scented rose petals add a subtle fragrance and taste — make sure the petals are fresh, unblemished and organic. Straight from your garden is best; do not use petals from a commercially grown rose.

Ingredients
2 red peppers
2 large red chillies
1 garlic clove, crushed
$\frac{1}{4}$ tsp coriander seeds
$\frac{1}{2}$ tsp caraway seeds
$2\frac{1}{2}$ tbsp olive oil plus extra for storing (optional)
A few scented rose petals (optional)

1 Cook and skin the peppers and chillies (see page 90).
2 Chop the flesh, discarding the stalk, seeds and membranes.
3 Blend to a paste with the remaining ingredients.

The trusty basics
Clockwise, from top: Cinnamon, ground ginger, cloves, turmeric, crushed red chilli, cardamom. You can't go wrong with these!

 171 Indian masalas

In India, blending spices into a masala (the Indian name for a combination of spices in the form of a powder or paste) is made even more complex due to regional diversity. The spices to keep on hand include mustard, coriander, cumin, peppercorns, cardamom, cinnamon, cloves, nutmeg, turmeric and chilli flakes. Garam masala, used as a seasoning for finishing dishes, is a warming, fragrant combination of cardamom, cumin, cinnamon, nutmeg, cloves and black pepper, sometimes with coriander added. It's one to experiment with.

172 Best-before dates

How you store spices makes a big difference to their staying power — find a cool, dry, dark location, as far from the heat and steam of the working end of the kitchen as possible, and store them in an airtight jar. Ground spices are very convenient, but they lose their flavour more rapidly than whole ones. A best-before date is only a guide — your best indication of whether a spice is still fresh is to sniff. If the aroma fails to get your gastric juices flowing, it's time to replace the spice.

Nuts and seeds

Now that nuts and seeds have been recognized as an excellent source of 'good' fats and beneficial for almost everything, there's every reason to make liberal use of them in cooking.

173   The fab five

These are the most versatile nuts for cooking — it's amazing how easily they align themselves with meat, fish, vegetables and baking ingredients.

Almonds The creamy texture and sweet flavour works in both savoury and sweet recipes, from chilled almond soup to luscious no-flour cakes. Buy flaked almonds ready prepared (it's hard to do yourself); otherwise, choose whole nuts and chop or grind them yourself. To blanch, cover in boiling water, drain when the skins loosen and squeeze out the nuts.

Hazelnuts These are at their best lightly toasted in the oven, when they make a delicious garnish for salads, a crust for meat and fish or a stuffing for vegetables. They're also excellent in baking. To skin, toast lightly in the oven until golden and the skins will slip off easily. Hazelnut oil makes a delectable salad dressing.

Walnuts These sweet, moist nuts are the simple choice — they're at their best raw, don't need skinning and are easy to chop with a sharp knife. They can become bitter when overcooked, but are wonderful lightly toasted. They're more forgiving when not exposed directly to heat, so they work well in walnut sauces and in baking. Walnut oil is divine.

Pistachios The prettiest of all nuts — blanch them in the same way as almonds to reveal their gorgeous green colour. They're used in both savoury and sweet dishes in Middle Eastern, Indian and Italian cuisine.

Cashews Not a genuine nut, but a nut-like seed. They work really well in stir-fries, curries and stuffings and are delicious toasted and added to salads. Despite their sweet flavour and creamy, crumbly texture, they're not the most obvious choice for sweet dishes, yet they're lovely in biscuits and make an excellent dairy-free base for ice cream.

174 Loved all over the world

Sesame seeds are used worldwide in cooking — in their natural state or as sesame oil, or ground into tahini, a paste used in Middle Eastern dishes. A jar of tahini in the cupboard opens up all sorts of possibilities — hummus and *baba ghanoush*, of course, but also

a great sauce for drizzling. To make the sauce, whisk 5 tablespoons of tahini with the juice of a lemon, then whisk in 4–5 tablespoons of water — until the consistency appeals to you — and season to taste with sea salt. Add a crushed garlic clove if you like. Blending the whole thing with a small bunch of parsley until smooth makes a pretty, pale green sauce full of zingy flavour.

Enriching addition
Tahini sauce is an excellent way to add protein, vitamins and minerals to a vegetable-based dish. If you're feeling adventurous, try using black tahini.

175 Toasted pine nuts

These tiny, pale, creamy little pseudo nuts are a key ingredient in pesto Genovese, and also enhance salads (try adding a few to tabbouleh). Toasting them brings out their flavour but is a delicate operation as they burn very easily. They're naturally very oily, so dry-toast them in a pan or in the oven and keep a watchful eye.

> **TRY IT**
>
> **Peanut butter** This pseudo nut is actually a legume, hence its name. In cooking, it really comes into its own as peanut butter — in cookies, and in spicy Asian sauces such as satay (great with chicken and beef) and gado-gado (a vegetarian favourite served with tofu, eggs and vegetables).

176 Egyptian Dukkah

Dukkah is a versatile spiced nut and seed mix. Sprinkle a spoonful on salads, soups, grains, roasted roots or your favourite dip, or serve with bread and olive oil for dunking. It's also delicious as a rub for meat and fish or in a marinade. Recipes vary in complexity, but a good basic mix is 250 g (9 oz) sesame seeds, 125 g (4 oz) coriander seeds, 60 g (2 oz) cumin seeds and 60 g (2 oz) hazelnuts. Lightly toast the seeds and nuts in a dry frying pan or a hot oven (separately, as they'll colour at a different rate), then grind the whole mix with sea salt and black pepper, using a pestle and mortar. Try including sunflower seeds, almonds, fennel seeds and a pinch of dried thyme — it's a recipe to have fun with.

Crunchy topping
Dukkah works its magic as a dry mix with texture, not a paste, so don't be tempted to add oil.

Know your oils

Oils are a by-product of foods that emerge from the ground. They are an essential part of all cuisines, from the cheap seed oils used for cooking to the exquisite nut oils and single-estate olive oils that should never go near a frying pan.

177 Experiment with vinaigrette

Salad leaves need a tasty oil-and-vinegar dressing. And it's so easy to make (see steps, right). A good basic combo is extra virgin olive oil and white wine vinegar, but there are endless variations. Try these:

- Avocado oil and raspberry vinegar
- Walnut oil and sherry vinegar
- Pumpkin seed oil and balsamic vinegar

1 Use 3 tablespoons oil and 1 tablespoon vinegar or lemon juice, seasoned to taste with salt and pepper. Add a teaspoon or so of clear honey if you like.

178 Hot and cold pressing

Oil is extracted from its source by pressing, with or without the help of heat. The most flavourful, and most expensive, oils are cold-pressed and derived from the first pressing. 'Extra virgin' oils, as these are known, are best reserved for dipping, drizzling and dressings. Oil from subsequent pressing is milder, cheaper and adequate — and in some cases better — for cooking.

2 Whisk the ingredients vigorously with a balloon whisk. Alternatively, place the ingredients in a screw-cap glass jar, screw on the lid — very firmly — and shake vigorously.

TRY IT

Oil-pouring spout
A narrow spout that fits into the neck of the bottle makes it far easier to deliver a drizzle of oil, rather than an out-of-control glug. Alternatively, decant the oil into a tin with a long spout.

3 All that whisking has caused the oil and vinegar to emulsify. It won't last, so if you're making the vinaigrette in advance, it'll need another whisk/shake before you use it.

The right oil for the job

SAUTÉ	Virgin olive, coconut, groundnut (peanut), grapeseed, sunflower, avocado
ROAST	Virgin olive, rapeseed, grapeseed, avocado
SIZZLE	Rapeseed, grapeseed, sunflower, safflower, groundnut, light sesame, avocado
MARINATE	Virgin olive, rapeseed, groundnut, avocado
DRESS	Extra virgin olive, rapeseed, grapeseed, avocado, pumpkin, toasted sesame, walnut, hazelnut, argan
DRIZZLE	Extra virgin olive, avocado, pumpkin, toasted sesame, walnut, hazelnut, argan

179 DIY oil infusions

Olive oil infused with flavour is more intense than just the sum of its parts. There are plenty of commercial infused oils available, but it's fun to make your own. Use a good but mild oil to allow the flavouring to come through.

Herb (basil, rosemary, thyme, marjoram, fennel, tarragon) Rinse, dry thoroughly and lightly bruise the herbs. Pack into a wide-mouthed jar, add the oil and cover the jar with muslin. Set aside in a warm (not hot) place for two weeks, stirring the mixture daily with a wooden spoon. Strain into a clean, dry bottle with a stopper.

Lemon zest Peel a washed and dried unwaxed lemon and set the peel aside, pith side up, to dry out. Place in a jar with a tight-fitting lid, cover with oil and infuse for two weeks. Alternatively, thinly pare the zest (see page 93), place in a pan with 250 ml oil and infuse over a very low heat for 15 minutes. Cool completely before removing the zest.

Garlic Place six fat garlic cloves in a pan with 250 ml oil and infuse over a very low heat for 1 hour. Cool completely before removing the garlic. Alternatively, place a whole bulb (see page 99), cut-side down, in a roasting pan, cover with foil and roast at 150°C (300°F) for 45 minutes. Strain the oil before bottling.

Chilli Place 2 teaspoons of chilli flakes in a pan with a small dried red chilli and 250 ml olive oil and infuse over a very low heat for 4 minutes. Transfer to a bottle and set aside in a cool, dark place, shaking the bottle regularly, until it reaches the level of heat you like.

180 Smoke point

Each oil has an individual 'smoke point' — the temperature at which it literally starts to smoke. So if you need to fry something over a high heat, choose an oil with a high smoke point. As a general rule, the more refined the oil, the higher its smoke point — which is why unrefined oils such as extra virgin olive oil are not recommended for high-temperature cooking. Butter has an even lower smoke point than olive oil, so a good tip when sautéing in butter is to add a little olive oil to prevent the butter from burning.

DAIRY

Dairy ingredients are often an unobtrusive element in a dish. We admire the meat, the fish, the vegetables, but who really notices the egg that holds a burger together, the butter that enhances a cod fillet, the cream that mellows a tomato sauce? This chapter explores the work of this gorgeous produce.

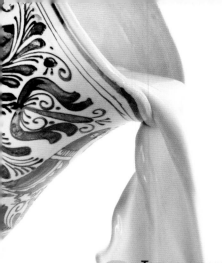

Understanding dairy ingredients

What exactly do dairy ingredients do? They're delicious in their own right, or as an accompaniment, but they have all sorts of clever qualities that offer remarkable support to other ingredients.

181 Temperamental cream

Cream is the luxury ingredient in both savoury and sweet cooking, but it can be unstable and separate or curdle at high temperatures, although the higher the fat content, the more forgiving it is.

Single cream This has a relatively low fat content so will not whip, but it's great for adding a touch of joy to sauces, soups and savoury dishes, and for pouring and swirling. Single cream curdles at high temperatures, so let the sauce cool before adding the cream, and do not bring it to a boil if reheating.

Soured cream This is single cream soured using a culture. It's much thicker than single cream so is great for dips and adding to soups and casseroles, and is also used in baking.

Crème fraîche This is a richer, thicker type of soured cream. Full-fat crème fraîche doesn't curdle or separate at high temperatures, which makes it perfect for cooking.

Whipping cream Depending on the fat content, whipping cream might collapse quickly so it's best used immediately once whipped. It's also good for pouring.

Double cream Rich and delicious, double cream doubles in volume when whipped and the fat globules trap the air, creating the light texture. If you want your cream to stay whipped, this is the one to use.

182 Cheese — pure umami

Cheese was one of the original foods identified for its umami qualities. The more 'aged' the cheese, the richer the umami, and an aged Parmesan tops the bill. Cheese comes in many forms, from soft to hard, from crumbly to rubbery, and each type behaves differently when cooked (see page 121 for uses of some of the most famous). In some recipes it melts and almost disappears, leaving only its taste; in others, it bakes or grills to a delectable golden brown. It's worth exploring its diversity.

183 Flavoursome yoghurt

Yoghurt is made from fermented milk and at a pinch can be used in recipes as a substitute for cream or crème fraîche. Use yoghurt without any additives and made from whole milk for the best flavour, and add it at the end of cooking to avoid curdling. It's also good in dressings and marinades, and in baking.

Back to basics
There's a satisfying simplicity to dairy ingredients. Cottage cheese, for example, is so called because it was traditionally made at home.

184 The versatile egg

Even though they're not milk-related, eggs are classed as 'dairy'. They work as a standalone item that can be cooked in a huge variety of ways. They also add a rich flavour to other ingredients and have a coagulant effect, making them useful for binding stuffings and burgers as well as helping coatings such as nuts or breadcrumbs adhere to fish, vegetables, etc. Separated into its constituent parts, the yolk thickens sauces, whereas beaten whites are full of trapped air, which adds volume.

185 Marvellous milk

Although other dairy ingredients might have more stage presence than the milk from which they're made, milk is a key ingredient in cooking. It's essentially just a form of liquid, but one that comes ready equipped with a unique flavour and richness. The obvious use for milk is in sauces and soups, but it also serves as a meat tenderizer, enriches baked goods and puts a creamy slant on grains. Use whole milk in cooking — the fat content is what provides milk with taste and body.

186 Mmmmm ... butter

Butter is very high in fat and makes everything taste delicious — there's simply no substitute for it in savoury dishes, with vegetables and in baking. Unsalted is best for cooking as it gives you control of the salt content.

The joy of eggs

Eggs are surely the most versatile of all foods — they take up so little space but do so many clever things for a relatively low cost, even for the best-quality organic free-range specimens.

187 Storage

Store eggs in the refrigerator, or a cool, dry place. It's easiest to separate eggs straight from the refrigerator (see page 115), but bring them to room temperature for everything else.

188 The fresh test

A fresh egg has a firm, plump yolk that holds its shape and does not leak into the white. To test an egg for freshness, lower it into a glass of water.

Fresh The egg sinks to the bottom of the glass and remains there. If you're using a recipe that includes raw eggs, they must pass this freshness test.

Less fresh If the egg settles halfway down the glass, it's less fresh but still usable.

Stale An egg that floats on top of the water is past its best-before date and should be discarded.

TRY IT

Easy peeling Hard-boiled fresh eggs are harder to peel than older ones, but fresher is better. To peel a hard-boiled egg, first roll it around under your palm on a work surface. This cracks the shell all over and makes it much easier to remove.

3 Golden rules — 189 The perfect omelette

1 Bring the eggs to room temperature — eggs straight from the refrigerator will take longer to set and speed is of the essence.

2 Use the right-size frying pan — too large and the omelette will set too quickly and be flat and leathery; too small and the bottom will set quickly and become rubbery while the rest of the omelette is struggling to cook.

3 Make sure the frying pan is hot enough — if in doubt, test it by sprinkling in a few drops of cold water, which should skitter and sizzle immediately.

5 Reasons — 190 to keep some eggs in your fridge

1 Heat some frozen spinach nuggets and serve with poached or fried eggs for a high-speed snack.

2 Add an egg to leftover risotto, mashed potato, crushed chickpeas or whatever you have, to make burgers.

3 Use up odds and ends of veggies in a frittata.

4 Make pancakes or crêpes for a lazy weekend brunch.

5 Always be prepared for an impromptu baking session.

191 How to achieve the world's lightest, fluffiest omelette

An omelette can be a fluffy, melting delight or something that doubles as a Frisbee. The secret to lightness lies in cooking the omelette quickly in the right-size frying pan — less than a minute for a 2-large or 3-medium egg omelette in a 23 cm (9-inch) pan. Use fresh, well-flavoured eggs and a small, nonstick pan with sloping sides for ease of serving.

1 Beat the eggs with a fork or whisk until just mixed then season to taste with salt and pepper.

2 Meanwhile, place the frying pan over a medium-high heat — it needs to be hot enough to set the base of the omelette within seconds. Drizzle in a little olive oil followed by a generous knob of unsalted butter. Swirl the pan to coat the base evenly.

3 Pour in the eggs and shake the frying pan to settle them. Cook them, undisturbed, until they start to bubble.

4 Draw the edges of the omelette into the centre with a fork and shake the pan so that the uncooked egg flows back out to the edges. The finished omelette should still jiggle a little in the centre.

When it's done
If an omelette 'jiggles' in the middle it means it's no longer runny but nor is it completely set.

Egg ID

Source		Characteristics	Notes
Hen	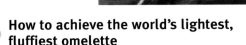	Shell colour varies, depending on breed of hen; yolk colour varies with diet; commercially produced eggs are graded into sizes.	For best flavour, use organic, free-range eggs; the shell colour does not affect the flavour of the egg.
Duck		Slightly larger than hen eggs; shell colour varies but sometimes a pretty 'duck-egg blue'; yolk colour varies with diet.	Duck eggs are more porous than hens' so store carefully to avoid contamination.
Goose		Larger than duck eggs; whitish shell; rich, creamy, flavourful yolk.	One medium goose egg is equivalent to two large hen eggs.
Quail		About a quarter the size of hen eggs, with a higher proportion of yolk to white; brown, speckled shell; rich flavour, delicate texture.	Quail eggs cook very quickly — only 30 seconds to soft-boil; reserve them for cooking methods that show off their size.

30 ways to serve an egg, global-style

1

2

5

8

15

16

17

18

19

20

22

1 *Fried*

2 *Huevos rancheros (Mexican fried eggs)*

3 *Uova in purgatorio ("eggs in purgatory")*

4 *Pisto con huevos (ratatouille with eggs)*

5 *Poached*

6 *Eggs Benedict*

7 *Eggs Florentine*

8 *Coddled (en cocotte)*

9 *Shirred*

10 *Shakshouka (Middle Eastern baked eggs)*

11 *Scrambled*

12 *Piperade (Basque scrambled eggs)*

13 *Zarangollo (Spanish scrambled eggs)*

14 *Anda bhurji (Indian scrambled eggs)*

15 *Steamed*

16 *Omelette*

17 *Soufflé omelette*

18 *Tortilla*

19 *Frittata*

20 *Tamagoyaki (Japanese omelette)*

21 *Kai jeow (Thai omelette)*

22 *Egg-fried rice*

23 *Boiled (hard/soft)*

24 *Scotch eggs*

25 *Chinese marbled tea eggs*

26 *Kedgeree*

27 *Chinese egg drop soup*

28 *Stracciatella (Italian egg drop soup)*

29 *Avgolemono (Greek egg and lemon soup)*

30 *Changua (Colombian egg and milk soup)*

24

25

26

29

193 Successful separation

Separating eggs is quite a skill. Use very fresh eggs, straight from the refrigerator (the cool temperature firms the yolk). Separate each egg into two bowls before adding the yolk and whites to the ones you've already done — this way, if the yolk splits into the white, you've only wasted one egg. Try these separation methods:

Egg separator This gadget has a narrow slit through which the white slips out, leaving the yolk behind. There's also a pipette version — crack the egg into the bowl, then suck out the yolk, which remains whole.

Shell Crack open the egg widthways and release most of the white into a bowl, without losing the yolk. Now transfer the yolk from one half of the shell to the other, each time tipping out the white, until only the yolk remains.

Fingers Crack open the egg, pour the contents into the palm of one hand and transfer the egg from one hand to the other, letting the white slide through your fingers into a bowl.

194 Freezing eggs

Eggs can be frozen for up to three months. Thaw in the refrigerator and use immediately. If you've frozen the eggs in a freezer bag, transfer them into a bowl and cover with cling film to thaw, to avoid mess and waste. Remember to mark the bag/box with the number of whole eggs/ yolks/whites.

• Break whole eggs into a bowl and beat them lightly, then pour into a resealable freezer bag or an airtight freezer box.

• Beat egg yolks lightly with a pinch of salt or sugar (depending on intended use) to prevent thickening. Freeze as for whole eggs.

• No preparation needed for egg whites; simply tip into the freezer bag or box.

Authentic Spanish tortilla

Omelettes are usually a quick fix but a tortilla, properly made, takes about an hour. It's worth every minute of the wait.

Ingredients
2 large onions, finely chopped
500 g (18 oz) waxy new potatoes, cut into 2.5 cm (1-inch) chunks
1 red chilli, seeded and chopped
1 garlic bulb, cloves separated and peeled
Olive oil, for cooking
12 eggs
Salt and pepper
Large bunch of parsley, chopped
Sprigs of thyme and tarragon, leaves stripped off and chopped

1 Place the onion, potatoes, chilli and garlic in a large frying pan and cover completely with olive oil. Cook over a medium heat for 20 minutes, or until the potatoes are cooked through but not browned.
2 Remove the frying pan from the heat and transfer the contents carefully into a strainer set over a bowl to drain off the oil. Wipe the pan with kitchen paper.
3 Beat the eggs, season generously with salt and pepper, and stir in the chopped herbs.
4 Place the frying pan over a low heat and pour in half the egg mixture. Arrange the potato mixture on top and cover with the remaining eggs.
5 Cook for 15–20 minutes, until the tortilla is almost set, then loosen the edges with a palette knife. Place a plate over the frying pan, invert the pan to turn out the tortilla, then slide it back into the pan and cook for an additional 5 minutes until it's firm on the outside but still moist on the inside. Let rest for a few minutes before serving.

Sweet eggs

Delicious egg-based desserts such as ice cream and crème brûlée start with a silky smooth custard infused with flavoursome, aromatic vanilla seeds. Transform the egg whites left over after making custard into melt-in-the-mouth meringues. Double heaven!

A spoonful of heaven

The trick with custard-making is to take your time. Rush the process and you risk ending up with a lumpy mess more akin to scrambled eggs than a silky custard.

Ingredients

600 ml double cream
1 vanilla pod, split lengthways
6 large egg yolks, at room temperature
2 tbsp caster sugar

1 Place the cream in a pan and add the vanilla pod — the seeds will float out as the cream heats. You can use vanilla powder instead, or even vanilla extract, although this lacks the visual appeal of seeds or powder.
2 Bring the cream slowly to boiling point, stirring occasionally, then simmer for 1 minute. Remove from the heat, cover and set aside for 10 minutes to infuse.
3 Reheat the cream to just under boiling point while you whisk the egg yolks with the sugar. Remove the vanilla pod.
4 Temper the egg yolks with a little of the hot cream, whisking constantly, then whisk in the remaining cream.

FIX IT

Curdling calamity? Rescue curdled custard by chilling it rapidly (dunk the pan in cold water), passing it through a sieve into a blender, then whizzing until smooth. But prevention is better than cure — remember to temper the eggs, then keep the heat low as the custard thickens to prevent it from boiling.

195 Simply the best

To transform the custard base into ice cream, increase the sugar content to 5 tbsp. Strain the custard into a clean pan and place on a low heat, stirring constantly with a wooden spoon, until the custard coats the back of the spoon. Strain into a chilled bowl, refrigerate to chill completely and churn in an ice-cream maker. Alternatively, pour the chilled custard into a shallow freezer box and freeze until it begins to firm up around the edges, then transfer it into a bowl and beat until smooth. Return to the freezer and repeat the process once or twice before leaving to freeze completely.

3 Golden rules

196 Freezing ice cream

1 Using icing sugar instead of caster sugar in the custard base will speed up the freezing process considerably.

2 The taste will change: once frozen, the custard base tastes less sweet.

3 Adding alcohol to ice cream stops it freezing completely hard.

CRÈME BRÛLÉE FLAVOUR COMBOS

The classic crème brûlée is flavoured simply with vanilla, but you can have fun adding herbs, citrus zest, flowers or flower water, chocolate ... Try these:

Rosemary ✚ orange zest

Lavender ✚ lime zest

Rose water ✚ white chocolate

197 Crème de la crème

To bake the custard for crème brûlée:

1 Place individual ramekins in a roasting pan. Strain the custard through a fine sieve into a jug, then strain again into the ramekins.

2 Pour boiling water into the roasting pan to come halfway up the ramekins and place in a preheated oven (170°C/325°F) for 12–15 minutes, until a skin forms on the custard but the custard still jiggles slightly.

3 Remove immediately from the roasting pan, allow to cool, then chill in the refrigerator for several hours before adding the topping.

A perfect crème brûlée topping splinters with a satisfying 'crack' when tapped with a teaspoon. To achieve this, sprinkle a thin, even layer of caster sugar (6 mm/¼ inch) over the chilled custard base. Caramelize the sugar using a chef's blowtorch, or half-bury the ramekins in crushed ice in a roasting pan and place under a very hot grill. Chill the crème brûlée again for 1 hour then serve immediately.

TRY IT

Not quite ice cream *Semifreddo* ('half-frozen') has a melting, mousse-like texture and is a great substitute for ice cream. It's made from the same ingredients but needs no cooking or churning. It can be flavoured simply with vanilla or dressed up with cherries or berries, chopped or grated chocolate, or crushed praline, torrone or amaretti. Freeze it in a loaf tin lined with cling film — this makes it easy to turn out, and it slices neatly for serving.

Beating egg whites

Egg whites, when whisked, transform from an unmanageable viscous blob to a bowlful of foam many times the volume. They are used to make soufflés (see page 123), meringues (see right) and mousses, and to add structure and lightness to flour-free cakes.

1 Use a copper, glass or stainless steel bowl and a hand balloon whisk or electric whisk. Make sure the equipment is absolutely clean, dry and grease-free. Any hint of grease will cause the foamy egg whites to collapse.

2 Whisk the room-temperature egg whites gently until frothy, then add a pinch of cream of tartar or 2 drops of lemon juice or vinegar to stabilize and add volume to the whites. You don't need to do this if your bowl is copper.

3 Beat vigorously until the whites form soft peaks when you lift out the whisk. If the recipe calls for stiff peaks, keep going, but beware — if you overdo it, the whites become dry and unstable and it's also harder to incorporate them into the base mixture. Use immediately.

The gravity test
When egg whites are properly whisked, they should stay firmly in place when you turn the bowl upside down. Be brave and try it!

198   Folding in egg whites

Always fold egg whites gently into the base mixture to avoid losing volume. Start by adding a large spoonful of the whisked egg whites to loosen the base mixture, then add the rest. Rotate the bowl with one hand while folding in the whites with the other, using a large tablespoon, in a constant up-and-over circular motion. Twist your wrist at the top of the circle so the bowl of the spoon always faces inwards.

199 Melting meringues

To make a basic meringue, simply whisk the egg whites to soft-peak stage (see left), then gradually add caster sugar (5 tablespoons/60 g/2 oz per large egg white), beating until the mixture is stiff and glossy. Form nests or shells on a baking sheet lined with baking parchment, place in a preheated oven (150°C/300°F) and reduce the temperature to 140°C (275°F). Bake for 30 minutes then switch off the oven and let the meringues dry out while the oven cools. Check the weather forecast before making meringues — they're more likely to fail in high humidity, because any moisture makes the mixture unstable.

200 The elegant art of the macaron

French macarons are both divine and daunting, but preparation and attention to detail are the keys to success.

1 Separate the egg whites a day or two ahead and let them stand in a loosely covered bowl at room temperature to dehydrate — this guarantees a chewy centre and a firm shell.
2 Measure the dry ingredients accurately — use icing sugar and finely ground almonds and sift them together before you start whisking the egg whites.

3 Whisk the egg whites to stiff peaks but remember not to overdo it.
4 Fold the sugar and almond mixture into the beaten egg whites quickly and lightly, in four batches.
5 When you've piped out the macarons, tap the baking sheet on the counter to eliminate air bubbles and settle the mixture.
6 Open the oven door for a few seconds halfway through cooking to release the steam.

201 Balsamic zabaglione

Zabaglione is a warm, light froth of a dessert. To avoid scrambling the eggs, make sure the water in the pan is barely simmering, use a bowl that sits well above the water and whisk constantly.

Ingredients
7 tbsp dessert wine
1 tbsp balsamic vinegar
1 egg
5 egg yolks
6 tbsp caster sugar

1 Combine the dessert wine and balsamic vinegar in a small jug.
2 Place the whole egg, egg yolks and sugar in a large heatproof bowl and place it over a saucepan of barely simmering water.
3 Using a balloon whisk or a handheld electric whisk, whisk until the mixture is thick and mousse-like.
4 Gradually add the wine/balsamic mixture, whisking constantly.
5 Remove the bowl from the heat and continue to whisk until the mixture is thick but light and smooth.

FIX IT

Meringues gone wrong?
Coarsely crush failed meringues and fold them into lightly whipped cream with chopped strawberries and strawberry purée. It's supposed to look like a mess, so imperfection is the goal!

TRY IT

Silicon macaron mould
This useful mould is marked with circles with a low rim or shallow indentations to hold the paste in place and create neat edges. Preheating the mould before piping out the paste helps set the foot of the macaron (the frilly base). Remember to place the mould on a baking sheet before piping out the paste, and let the cooked macarons cool completely before removing them.

Cheese connoisseur

The cheesemaker's skill is evident in the fact that varieties range from young and fresh to mature and even mouldy, albeit a controlled mould. Some cheeses are even 'protected', meaning they can only be produced by a certain method in a particular location. Cheese is a serious subject!

5 Reasons 202 to keep a hard cheese in your fridge

1 Grate and add to an omelette, scrambled eggs, etc.

2 Add to béchamel sauce to cloak vegetables such as cauliflower or to layer in baked dishes such as lasagne.

3 Toss cubed crustless bread with olive oil and grated cheese, season to taste and bake at 190°C (375°F) for 10 minutes, until crisp and golden. Scatter over soup or salad.

4 Blend in a food processor with roughly torn crustless bread, mixed dried herbs and a splash of olive oil to make a topping for fish, chicken, veggies, etc.

5 Add to béchamel sauce, spread on top of a toasted ham and cheese sandwich and grill until golden and bubbling for a croque-monsieur.

203 Storage

The best way to store cheese is to liberate it from its plastic wrapping and cover it in greaseproof paper, then aluminium foil, and keep it refrigerated. If you're serving it on its own, always bring it to room temperature for about an hour to bring out the flavour; however, it's easiest to grate or crumble it straight from the refrigerator for use in cooked dishes, sauces, etc. Unless it was intended to be 'blue' (that is, cheeses treated with the edible mould *Penicillium roqueforti*), any cheese that shows signs of mould should be discarded.

Balancing the board

An enticing cheese board needs a good blend of cheeses. Olives, celery and grapes (not too sweet) are an excellent foil for the cheese.

Offer hard cheeses from both ends of the strength scale

A ripe soft cheese, such as brie, is good for spreading

Vary the size and shape of the blocks offered to maximize visual appeal

Always include a blue, to cater to the stronger palate

Cheese ID

Most cheeses are excellent in salads or as part of a cheese board, but work equally well in cooked dishes. These are some of the most versatile from around the world.

Milk type	Name	Characteristics	Use for ...	Notes
Cow	Swiss (Emmental, Gruyère)	Firm, slightly rubbery texture with marble-size holes; distinctive nutty flavour	Fondues, gratins, quiches; good with fish	Grates well
	Cheddar	Hard cheese, texture and flavour vary with age from creamy and mild to flaky and sharp	Sauces, toppings, baking	Grates well
	Parmesan	Hard, grainy, crumbly texture; piquant, salty, umami-rich flavour	Pasta, risotto, sauces, baking	Best freshly grated or shaved; use the rind to flavour soups; very salty, adjust seasoning accordingly
	Blue (Stilton, Gorgonzola)	Blue-veined, crumbly; strong aroma, distinctive, pungent flavour	Salads, dressings, pasta, risotto	Blue cheese is also made with both sheep and goat's milk
	Paneer	Firm, dense-textured, unsalted Indian cheese; bland flavour	Curries, kebabs	Holds its shape when heated; marries well with strong flavours
Buffalo/cow	Mozzarella	Soft and white, with a firm texture, stringy when cooked; creamy, slightly sour flavour	Salads, with tomatoes and basil; pasta sauces, pizza toppings	Melts very easily
Sheep	Pecorino romano	Hard, grainy, crumbly texture similar to Parmesan; salty flavour	Use as Parmesan	Very salty, adjust seasoning accordingly
	Feta	White, firm, crumbly texture; salty flavour	Salads, pasta, pizza, stuffing vegetables	Very salty, adjust seasoning accordingly
	Halloumi	Very firm, springy texture; strong, salty flavour	Usually fried or grilled; makes excellent kebabs	High melting point, so keeps its shape extremely well
Goat	Hard or soft	Hard is firm and pale; soft is either very fresh, white and soft, or rinded with a creamy texture	Use hard as cheddar; soft in salads or for melting	

Mastering roux

The basis to many a sauce, a roux is a wonderful thing to have in your cooking arsenal, once you know how ...

Roux and béchamel

A roux is simply equal quantities of clarified butter (see page 126) and flour cooked together as a thickening agent for liquid. It differs from beurre manié (see page 127) in that it starts off a sauce, rather than completes it. The important thing is not to rush — your aim is to cook out the flour flavour without colouring the roux. Otherwise, béchamel sauce is very forgiving. Clarified butter gives a refined result, but ordinary butter will do. Ideally, warm the milk with aromatics — parsley stalks, a bay leaf, a garlic clove, a small shallot, a strip of lemon zest, a few black peppercorns — and set it aside to infuse for 30 minutes, but you can leave out this step if flavour doesn't matter too much. Here's how to make a classic béchamel, a versatile roux-based white sauce.

1 Heat 75 g (2½ oz) clarified butter in a heavy-based pan over a low heat until just melted, then add 75 g (2½ oz) plain flour.

2 Cook, whisking constantly with a balloon whisk, for about 5 minutes, until the mixture starts to froth. Meanwhile, heat 1 litre of milk to boiling point (or strain infused milk into a clean pan and reheat to boiling point).

3 Add half the milk to the roux a little at a time, beating constantly until any lumps disappear before adding more. Add the remaining milk and cook for 5 minutes to thicken the sauce, whisking occasionally.

Soufflé: The star of the show

Béchamel sauce opens up all sorts of recipe possibilities, not least of which is a light, melting soufflé — an impressive first course for dinner parties.

Ingredients

25 g (1 oz) butter
25 g (1 oz) plain flour
150 ml milk infused with aromatics
$\frac{1}{4}$ tsp mustard powder
Pinch of cayenne pepper
Salt and pepper, to taste
75 g ($2\frac{1}{2}$ oz) Gruyère cheese, grated
3 large eggs, separated

1 Make a béchamel sauce (see left) with the butter, flour and milk. Stir in the mustard powder and cayenne, season to taste and allow to cool slightly. Stir in the cheese.
2 Beat the egg yolks and beat them into the béchamel.
3 Whisk the egg whites to soft peaks. Beat 2 tbsp into the sauce, then fold in the rest (see page 118).
4 Transfer the mixture to a greased 850 ml soufflé dish, place on a baking tray and bake in a preheated oven (190°C/375°F) for about 30 minutes, until well risen and golden but still slightly wobbly in the centre. Serve immediately — soufflés collapse promptly.
5 Alternatively, bake in individual ramekins, greased and lined with baking parchment. Let the soufflés cool, then chill or freeze them. To reheat, remove from the dish, peel off the lining, place on a baking sheet lined with baking parchment and reheat in the oven at 190°C (375°F) for 10–15 minutes, until warm and puffy. These are called 'twice baked'.

205 No soufflé dish? Improvise!

A soufflé dish has depth to support the mixture as it rises. Any deep, straight-sided pan will work instead, such as a lined casserole or even a springform tin (encased in foil to prevent leaks). If necessary, add height with a baking parchment 'collar'. And if all else fails, use a cup.

TRY IT

Cheese soufflé tart Practise several cooking skills at once and make a cheese soufflé tart — the crisp pastry shell contrasts irresistibly with the soft soufflé filling. Add texture to the soufflé — asparagus and smoked fish work really well together.

Cream and butter

These are the truly indulgent dairy treasures — cream is made by skimming the fat off the milk, and butter is made by churning the cream. Cream and butter made from the milk of pasture-fed cows really is the crème de la crème.

206   Coeur à la crème

This is a slightly sweetened mixture of soft cream cheese, double cream and whisked egg whites, to serve with fruit. The 'coeur' in the name comes from the traditional heart-shaped moulds with a perforated base in which the mixture is drained in the refrigerator overnight, with a tray underneath to catch the whey. The trick is to line the moulds with a double layer of damp muslin (fold the excess tightly over the mixture), to facilitate turning out the set hearts.

207   Making mascarpone

Mascarpone — the Italian soft cheese that makes tiramisu so delectable — is very easy to make. In a stainless steel pan, gently heat 600 ml double cream to 80°C (175°F). Add a large pinch of tartaric acid and stir for 10 minutes, until curds form. Transfer to a sieve lined with muslin and set over a bowl to catch the whey. Let drain overnight in the refrigerator.

TRY IT

Crème chantilly Softly whipped double cream, chantilly is lightly sweetened with icing sugar and flavoured with vanilla seeds. Formed into quenelles (see page 155), it makes an elegant garnish for desserts.

New York cheesecake

A classic New York cheesecake is made from a rich cream cheese filling baked on a crumbly biscuit base, with a soured cream topping — an ambrosial use of dairy ingredients, and so easy when you know how.

Ingredients
Base
175 g (6 oz) graham crackers or digestive biscuits
75 g (2½ oz) unsalted butter, melted

Filling
300 g (10½ oz) cream cheese
60–75 g (2–2½ oz) caster sugar
2 large eggs
½ tsp vanilla extract
Finely grated zest of a lemon

Topping
300 g (10½ oz) soured cream
40 g (1½ oz) caster sugar
½ tsp vanilla extract

1 Place the biscuits in a resealable freezer bag and crush with a rolling pin to a breadcrumb consistency. Transfer to a bowl and stir in the butter. Line the base of a loose-based 18 cm (7 inch) layer cake tin with baking parchment and press the crumb mixture into the base. Chill in the refrigerator for 30 minutes.
2 Beat the filling ingredients together with a fork until smooth, but don't overdo it as too much air will make the filling crack. Pour over the chilled base and smooth the surface.
3 Place on a baking tray and bake in a preheated oven (190°C/375°F) for 25–30 minutes, until set but still slightly wobbly in the centre. Remove from the oven and allow to cool on a wire rack for 15 minutes. Meanwhile, increase the oven temperature to 240°C (475°F).
4 Combine the topping ingredients and pour over the cheesecake. Return to the oven for 10–12 minutes, until the topping is set and lightly browned around the edge. Set the tin on a wire rack and loosen the cheesecake from the sides of the tin with a round-ended table knife to prevent the surface cracking as it cools. Allow to cool completely in the tin, then chill in the refrigerator for several hours or overnight.

Sweet idea
A basic cheesecake recipe allows
for creativity. A rich, full-fat cream
cheese is a must, but try replacing
the caster sugar with light brown
sugar for a richer colour and hint
of toffee flavour.

208   Clarified butter

To 'clarify' butter means to remove the milk solids. The clear yellow liquid that remains has a higher smoke point, making it more forgiving for sautéing. It's also good for sauces. The clarification process removes impurities from the butter, extending its storage life in the refrigerator by several weeks, so it's worth making a big batch if you're likely to use it a lot. In India, where clarified butter is called 'ghee', the melted butter is simmered for 30 minutes, deepening the flavour and colour.

1 Chop unsalted butter into a heavy-based pan, place over a low heat and warm gently until completely melted.

2 A frothy layer of milky residue will have formed on top of the butter. Skim this off carefully with a ladle and discard it.

3 Very carefully pour off the clarified layer, leaving behind the layer of milk solids.

209   Beurre blanc

To make a *beurre blanc* sauce, bring 200 ml dry white wine to a boil in a small pan with a finely chopped shallot, then simmer until reduced by half. Strain into a heatproof bowl. Place the bowl over a pan of simmering water and whisk in 175 g (6 oz) diced unsalted butter, one piece at a time, until the sauce emulsifies. Season to taste.

Perfect partners
The slightly acidic flavour of beurre blanc offsets the sweetness of scallops.

5 Reasons

210

to keep a block of butter in your fridge

1 Combine with leftover white wine to make beurre blanc (see below left), a quick and easy emulsified sauce that transforms fish and seafood.

2 Beat until soft and creamy, add flavourings (see below right), roll in cling film to form a sausage and store in the refrigerator or freezer. Add slices to vegetables, fish and seafood, steak, risotto and toasted sourdough bread.

3 Make brown butter (see page 65) to pour over fish, vegetables or pasta.

4 Add to a sauce at the end of cooking to add gloss and richness.

5 For baking — nothing matches it for taste and texture.

---

211 Buttermilk (and what to use instead)

Originally a by-product of butter-making but now commercially cultured, buttermilk is the liquid of choice to promote rising in pancakes and baked goods such as scones and soda bread (see page 139). At a minimum temperature of 80°C (175°F), the high acid content in buttermilk reacts with alkaline baking soda to create carbon dioxide, which has a leavening effect, resulting in a tender crumb. If you have no buttermilk, yoghurt or soured cream will do the same (dilute 3:1 with milk if necessary), as will cream of tartar in milk (1 tbsp per 300 ml milk) or lemon juice or cider/white wine vinegar in milk (2 tbsp per 300 ml milk).

FIX IT

Quick thickener Rescue a watery stew, sauce or soup with *beurre manié*, a paste made of equal quantities of plain flour and soft butter. Add to simmering liquid a little at a time, stirring vigorously until incorporated before adding more. When the liquid is almost the thickness you want, bring it to a boil and simmer again briefly.

BUTTER FLAVOUR COMBOS

With flavoured butter, there's huge scope for invention to suit your taste preferences. Here are a few ideas to start you off:

Anchovy   +   lemon

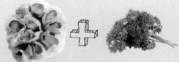

Roasted garlic   +   parsley

Red chilli   +   coriander   +   lime zest

BAKING

Baking is surely the most rewarding aspect of cooking. To assemble an assortment of unpromising-looking ingredients and then, by some strange scientific process, for those ingredients to emerge from the oven as a fragrant loaf, a crisp pastry or an irresistible cake is worth every minute of preparation.

Utensils and ingredients

Bakeware and ingredients have one thing in common — buy the best of both and you'll get the best results. Top-quality bakeware is something of an investment, but build up a collection and it will last a lifetime.

212 Bakeware essentials

Choose your bakeware with care and look after it lovingly — it's going to make all the difference to the success of your baking sessions.

Baking sheet For biscuits, cookies and free-form bread loaves and rolls. Invest in a sturdy one (cheaper ones warp in the oven) with three rimless edges for ease of removing the baked product.

Cake tins For layer cakes, fruitcakes and more. Again, go for heavy — cheaper tins are more likely to scorch the contents — and choose a springform tin or one with a removable base, as it's much easier to free the cake.

Loaf tin For bread, tea breads and loaf cakes.

Shallow tins For square cakes (brownies!), tarts, swiss rolls and roulades.

Mixing bowl Choose a roomy bowl with a wide top that enables you to get both hands in comfortably for rubbing butter into flour, gives you plenty of room to whisk egg whites, allows you to bring a large quantity of bread dough together ...

Sieve For sifting flour into the bowl from a great height to incorporate air.

Flexible dough scraper For mixing, transferring dough (bread, cookie, pie) from the mixing bowl to the work surface, scraping up stray bits, dividing, lifting.

Scales/measuring spoons Baking is a precise art, so equip yourself with kitchen scales and a set of measuring spoons ranging from $\frac{1}{8}$ teaspoon (0.5 ml) to 1 tablespoon (15 ml).

213 Squashy silicone

Hot to handle
Use a cloth to remove silicone moulds
from the oven — they get very hot.

Traditional cake tins must be greased and lined
with baking parchment every time they're used.
An easier option is nonstick silicone bakeware,
which only needs a spritz of nonstick cooking
spray. It squashes into a much smaller space
than traditional bakeware — useful if you have
limited storage.

214 Flour facts and types

Flour — usually made from wheat — is the base ingredient
in most baked goods. The type used depends on the
protein content.

Plain Made from a wheat variety that's relatively low in the
proteins that form gluten (see page 137), resulting in a light,
tender texture. It's the one to use for pastry, cakes and biscuits.
Self-raising Plain flour with added leavening (raising) agents.

Bread Made from more robust 'hard' wheat, which is high in
the proteins that form gluten, resulting in a chewy texture.

Gluten-free Blended from a variety of flours such as rice,
tapioca, potato and maize, for those who are gluten-intolerant.

215 Sugar facts and types

Sugar comes in several forms, each suitable for a different
baking purpose. If possible, choose a brand labelled 'unrefined'
for the best result in baking.

Caster sugar Fine, free-flowing grains. Refined crystals are
white, unrefined are pale gold. It's suitable for layer cakes,
sweet pastries and biscuits.

Light/dark brown Medium-sized, moist grains — they tend
to form solid lumps if they get damp. Brown sugar is used in
richer cakes such as fruitcake and gingerbread.

Icing sugar Very fine, powdered sugar, used mainly
for icing, frostings and buttercreams as it dissolves quickly,
and for dusting.

216 Does it still work?

To tell if your bicarbonate of soda (see page
141) is still active, stir ¼ tsp (1 ml) into a
mixture of 8 tbsp (½ cup) very hot water
and ¼ tsp (1 ml) vinegar — it should start
to bubble immediately. Use the same test
for baking powder, but without the vinegar.
This also works for self-raising flour, and
is the way to test whether that jar of
unlabelled flour is plain or self-raising. You
need to be confident that the flour is still
fresh — stale self-raising will not react.

FIX IT

Accurate temperature gauge
The actual oven temperature
doesn't always reflect what the
display is telling you, which
can lead to a baking
failure. If you suspect
this might be the
case with your
oven, use a
thermometer
as your guide.

217 A word about chocolate

Always use top-quality chocolate for recipes (70 percent minimum cocoa solids) and
unsweetened cocoa powder. To melt chocolate, chop it into small pieces and place it
in a heatproof bowl over a saucepan of barely simmering water — well above the water
level, or the chocolate will overheat and become grainy. Remove the bowl as soon as
the chocolate melts. Damp chocolate can 'seize' and refuse to melt, so store it in a cool
but dry place (not the refrigerator).

218 Honey, honey?

You can replace sugar with honey but
you'll need to adjust the recipe, using
only half to two-thirds the specified
amount of sugar, less liquid and a lower
oven temperature. Honey adds flavour
and gives a slightly heavier result.

The art of pastry

Pastry-making requires cool hands and a gentle touch — it's not something upon which to vent your frustrations! Originally invented solely as a vehicle for the filling, pastry has become so much more. Master it, and you're a baking star.

3 Golden rules

219 Shortcrust pastry

1 Chill the mixing bowl before you start, and use ice-cold water to mix the dough.

2 Chill the dough in the refrigerator for 30 minutes before rolling out — this relaxes the gluten strands, firms the butter and allows the moisture to settle out. Allow the dough to return to room temperature for 5–10 minutes before rolling.

3 Chill the prepared pastry shell in the refrigerator or freezer before baking — the aim is for the pastry to set in the oven before the butter starts to melt, so it must be very cold.

220 Get to know your butter

Some brands of butter soften quickly when you take them out of the refrigerator, whereas others are still solid an hour later. Pastry requires cold ingredients, but if using butter straight from the refrigerator means you have to work hard to rub it into the flour, disregard the rule and let it 'come to' at room temperature. If the butter starts to feel oily when you're rubbing it in, place the mixing bowl in the refrigerator for a few minutes.

TRY IT

Pastry blender If your hands tend to be warm, try using a pastry blender — this cuts the butter quickly, efficiently and evenly into the flour, without melting it. Remember to chill the blender before you start.

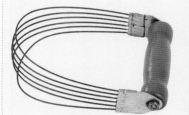

221 Crisp shortcrust

The key to successful pastry-making is to handle the ingredients as little as possible, so that the butter breaks down without melting completely, and the water is mixed in lightly to avoid overdeveloping the gluten in the flour — desirable in bread dough but toughens pastry dough. Chilling takes care of the rest (see below) and guarantees a light, crisp result.

Ingredients
200 g (7 oz) plain flour
Pinch of salt
100 g (3.5 oz) cold unsalted butter, cubed
Cold water, to mix

1 Sift the flour with the salt into a bowl, holding the sieve high to incorporate plenty of air for lightness.
2 Blend the butter into the flour — first with a flat-bladed table knife, using a cutting action, then finish rubbing it in quickly and lightly with your fingertips, lifting each handful high. The mixture should resemble breadcrumbs.
3 Sprinkle 2 tbsp (30 ml) water over the mixture and bring it together, first with the knife, then with your fingertips. Add more water if necessary, but only as much as needed to bring the dough together.

222 Rolling out

The best surface for rolling pastry dough is a marble slab, which keeps the dough cool and malleable. If you lack one of these, try a silicone mat marked with squares or concentric circles to use as a guide. Lightly flour the surface and the rolling pin. Flatten the pastry lightly with the rolling pin, then turn it and flatten again. Roll out using a backward-and-forward action in one direction, turning the pastry 90° every so often.

223   Uniting dough with tin

Lining Roll the pastry dough loosely around the rolling pin to lift it into the tart tin and ease it gently into the corners using a small ball of the dough — it's less likely to tear the dough than your fingers.

Trimming Allow the pastry dough to relax in the refrigerator for 10 minutes before trimming off the excess — the pastry is less likely to shrink in the oven.

Baking blind When lining the pastry shell with baking parchment for blind baking (see below), cut the parchment to the required size then crumple it tightly into a ball. Flatten it again and it'll mould gently into the shell without damaging the pastry.

224   Fragrant, spicy apple pie with a twist

Apple and cheese is a classic pairing and works wonderfully well in a pie — the cheese goes into the dough. Simply add a finely grated hard cheese, such as cheddar, to the blended flour and butter before adding the water — you'll need a quarter the combined weight, so for a 200 g (7 oz) flour/100 g (3½ oz) butter mix, add 7.5 g (2½ oz) cheese. Toss the apples with ground cinnamon for a fragrant finish.

225   Nobody likes a soggy bottom

Pre-baking a pastry shell 'blind' seals the pastry and prevents sogginess. Line the tart tin with dough, prick it all over with a fork and chill in the refrigerator for 30 minutes. Line the dough with baking parchment and baking beans. Bake for 20 minutes at 200°C (400°F), until the sides are set, then remove the beans and parchment. Brush the base with lightly beaten egg white and return to the oven for 5 minutes. Allow to cool completely before adding the filling. To help prevent a soggy double-crust pie, either sprinkle a thin layer of fine semolina on the base or brush it with lightly beaten egg white.

226 Flaky pastry

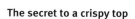

Flaky pastry is akin to puff pastry, but far less challenging for the novice cook to make.

Ingredients
225 g (8 oz) plain flour
Pinch of salt
160 g (5½ oz) unsalted butter

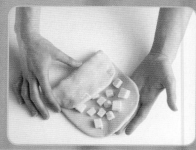

1 Make a pastry dough (see page 132) with the flour, salt and half the butter, and roll out to a 25 x 12.5 cm (10 x 5 inch) rectangle. Dot one-third of the remaining butter over the top two-thirds of the rectangle.

2 Fold the bottom third of the dough up and then carefully fold the top third down.

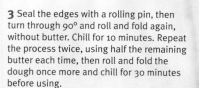

The secret to a crispy top
Make sure you seal the pastry firmly around the edge of the dish to trap the steam; if the steam escapes, the pastry might collapse into the filling and become soggy.

3 Seal the edges with a rolling pin, then turn through 90° and roll and fold again, without butter. Chill for 10 minutes. Repeat the process twice, using half the remaining butter each time, then roll and fold the dough once more and chill for 30 minutes before using.

227 Puff pastry

Puff pastry is the richest and lightest of all pastry types, created by alternating layers of pastry and butter. The preparation process, called 'lamination', is a long one, requiring much folding, rolling and turning (a good puff pastry has literally hundreds of layers), with periods of chilling between. When the pastry is cooked, the water in the butter layers turns to steam, causing the pastry to expand (puff). There's much to be said for cheating with this one, and buying a good brand of frozen all-butter puff pastry.

228 Creating borders

When making puff-pastry tarts or vol-au-vent cases, score a line with a sharp knife about 5 mm (¼ inch) from the edge of the shape, being careful not to cut all the way through. When you bake the pastry, the outer edge will create a raised border to anchor the filling in place.

TRY IT

Cheat's method You can cheat at flaky pastry by freezing the butter in foil until it's fairly solid, then grating it into the flour. Incorporate it using a flat-bladed table knife, then add water and complete as usual.

SAVOURY PUFF PASTRY FLAVOUR COMBOS

A puff-pastry tart is the ideal way to use up all the odds and ends in the refrigerator, and no one will guess that that's what you've done! Here are some suggestions for ingredients that go well together:

Soft goat's cheese + tomato + tapenade

Roast chicken + spinach + red pesto

Prosciutto + Emmental + artichoke

5 Reasons 229 to keep puff pastry in your freezer

1 Make a savoury tarte tatin (try red onion, beetroot or tomato) or a sweet one (apple, pear, apricot).

2 Encase a salmon fillet in puff pastry to make salmon en croute or *coulibiac*.

3 Fill with a butternut squash, mushroom, blue cheese and sage stuffing to make a vegetarian Wellington.

4 Bake vol-au-vent cases and stuff with a variety of fillings for a retro buffet.

5 Make novelty pie pops — cut out small circles, place a spoonful of filling on each (make a dry filling, as for ravioli) and insert a cake pop stick into the filling. Cover with a second circle and bake.

Dreamily creamy

Vols-au-vent cry out for a creamy filling. Either use real cream (double, soured, etc.) or make a light sauce to embrace the other ingredients.

Baking bread

Bread-making is a slow, relaxed process, from the long, rhythmic kneading to the rise, when the dough magically expands — but there are quick methods, too. There's nothing as enticing as the aroma of freshly baked bread!

Fail-safe bread dough

A basic bread dough is the start of your bread-making adventure.

Ingredients
1 kg (35 oz) strong white bread flour, or 600 g (21 oz) wholemeal and 400 g (14 oz) strong white bread flour
2 tsp active dry yeast
4 tsp salt
700 ml warm water

1 Place the flour in a large mixing bowl, stir in the yeast and rub in the flour with your fingertips. Stir in the salt. Add most of the water and mix it in.

2 Add the remaining water and bring the dough together — there should be no loose flour remaining in the bowl. Turn out the dough onto a clean work surface and knead for 5–10 minutes (see opposite).

3 Place the dough in a clean, lightly floured mixing bowl. Lightly flour the surface, cover with a cloth and set aside to rise until doubled in volume.

4 Turn out the dough, knead and shape. Cover with a tea towel, leave until doubled in volume, and bake at 230°C (450°F) — 30–40 minutes for a loaf, 12–15 minutes for rolls.

A matter of taste
If you like your bread crusty, let it cool uncovered. If you want a soft crust, let it cool under a clean tea towel.

231 Yeast: A useful fungus

Yeast is a microscopic fungus that reacts with sugar to produce carbon dioxide through fermentation. There are two methods of leavening bread using yeast.

Yeast This is used either in its fresh form, or — more readily available — in a dried granular form, either active dry or instant. Although fresh yeast gives the best flavour, active dry yeast is convenient and the most popular.

Wild yeast This is present in the atmosphere and is harnessed as a 'starter' to make what is known as sourdough bread (see page 139). Once you've created the starter (it takes about five days to develop and a month to mature), you can 'feed' it to use again, as often as you like — this is the method for the dedicated bread enthusiast.

232 Salt — who needs it?

Your bread does! Salt reinforces the gluten structure of the dough, which would otherwise be sticky and unstable, and regulates the rate of fermentation. If you're proofing the yeast, be sure to add the salt to the flour, not the yeast mixture, as it will kill the yeast.

233 Kneading — how it's done

Unless you have a mixer with a dough hook attachment, kneading is hard work — but it's also therapeutic and rewarding. The dough is frustratingly sticky to start with, but once you've stretched and rolled and turned it for a few minutes, the gluten starts to develop and before long (about 10 minutes) you have a smooth, silky dough.

234 Do you need to knead?

Wheat flour contains proteins called glutenin and gliadin, which develop into gluten molecules when mixed with water. The point of kneading is to organize the strands of gluten into a strong, elastic web that will trap the gas created by the yeast. A good test of whether the dough has been kneaded enough is to test its internal temperature with a meat thermometer — when it reaches 23°C (73°F), it's ready to rise.

235 Temperature and flavour

Bread recipes often tell you to put the dough in a warm place to rise, but in fact a fast rise is only desirable if you're in a hurry. The cooler the environment, the slower the rise — and the better the flavour. Bread dough will even rise in the refrigerator.

236 The hollow sound test

To test whether a loaf of bread is cooked through, turn it over and tap the base — if it sounds hollow, it's done.

1 Decant the dough onto a lightly floured work surface and flatten it a little.

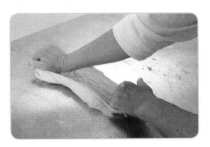

2 In one smooth, continuous movement, stretch the dough away from you with the heel of your hand, then roll it up towards you. Give the dough a quarter turn.

3 Repeat the stretching, rolling and turning action until the dough is smooth.

Baking stone

A great tool to own for bread-making is a really thick baking stone. To avoid 'shocking' the stone, put it in a cold oven and let it heat up with the oven. The stone holds heat really efficiently, helping to cook the bread from the underside up.

TRY IT

Magic mist Give the oven a spritz of mist from a spray bottle before putting in bread dough to bake. This keeps the atmosphere humid for a while and gives the bread time to rise unhindered before the crust forms.

237 Crisp, warm baguettes to fill with your favourite things

Make a batch of bread dough (see page 136) — ideally using French T55 flour for authenticity, or substitute a 50/50 mix of strong white bread flour and plain flour. The important thing is NOT to knead the dough after the rise — you want to retain the air bubbles, so simply cut the dough into pieces, spread each into a rectangle and roll gently into shape. You can create furrows in a tea towel to retain the shape as the baguettes rise, then transfer them to a baking sheet to bake, but your best ally is a perforated mould, which both shapes the baguettes and promotes a crisp crust as they bake. Use a razor or craft knife to make slashes in the top of the baguettes.

238 Soda bread for emergencies (and because it's wonderful)

Soda bread takes literally minutes to assemble, requires no kneading or proving and goes well with everything. It's best eaten on the day of baking, but you can halve the quantities to make a smaller loaf. There's no yeast in soda bread — the rise and crumb rely on the interaction between the bicarbonate of soda and buttermilk (see page 127).

Ingredients

250 g (9 oz) wholemeal flour, plus extra for dusting
250 g (9 oz) plain flour
1 tsp bicarbonate of soda
1 tsp salt
1 tbsp unsalted butter
420 ml buttermilk
(see page 127 for alternatives)

1 Combine the flour, bicarbonate of soda and salt in a large bowl and rub in the butter. Stir in the buttermilk and mix to a sticky dough.

239 The secret of sourdough

The key ingredient in sourdough bread is the 'starter'. Allow a month or so for this to mature. Place 75 g (2½ oz) organic wholemeal flour in a large airtight jar and stir in 5 tablespoons warm filtered water. Seal the jar and set aside in a warm place for 24 hours. Add the same quantity of water and flour, stirring vigorously, on each of the next three days, and by the fifth day you should see tiny air bubbles. Now transfer it to the refrigerator, but stir and feed it weekly, as above. Before using it, bring to room temperature for a day, then take out what you need for your recipe and feed what's left. Managed carefully, it should last indefinitely — we're talking years here!

TRY IT

Kneadless loaf A wholemeal 'Grant' loaf is made with yeast but it doesn't require kneading and only needs one 40-minute rise in a warm place. It's not suitable for free-form shaping or rolls — this one needs the support of a loaf tin.

Experiment with flour
Soda bread is often made with wholemeal flour, but you can use half wholemeal, half white or even all white, which makes a more elegant loaf — perfect for afternoon tea.

2 Turn the dough out onto a floured surface and roll it gently in the flour to form a ball. Place on a floured baking sheet and flatten slightly with your palm.

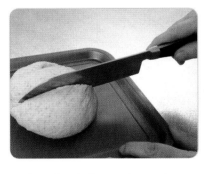

3 Using a sharp knife, score a cross-shape into the dough. Bake in a preheated oven (200°C/400°F) for 30 minutes, until risen and golden brown. Cool on a wire rack.

Cakes worth celebrating

A cake is a wonderful treat, and a homemade one is really special. No self-respecting celebration should be without a cake, and there's always a recipe to suit your mood, whatever the season or reason.

240 How to make a cake

Cakes are assembled by different methods, depending on the balance of ingredients.

Creaming (for cakes with a high proportion of butter) The butter is softened (not melted) and beaten with sugar, using a wooden spoon or electric whisk, until pale and fluffy. This makes a light, receptive base for incorporating the eggs with plenty of air. The flour is folded in last.

Rubbing-in (for cakes with a lower proportion of butter) The butter is rubbed lightly into the flour as for pastry dough, then the wet ingredients are added.

Melting (also used for cakes with a lower proportion of butter; easier than rubbing-in) The butter and sugar are melted together, then the eggs and any liquid are added, followed by the dry ingredients.

Whisking (for layer cakes with no butter) The egg yolks are whisked with sugar until very thick, then combined with stiff-peak egg whites and flour (or a flour substitute, such as ground almonds). Cakes made by this method need to be eaten as fresh as possible.

Good habit
Remember to switch on the oven before assembling and mixing your cake ingredients, so that it's up to temperature and ready to perform its magic.

241 Chemical reaction

Cakes made using the creaming method, where the eggs are added whole, usually call for baking powder or self-raising flour (sometimes both). Cakes made by the rubbing-in method require bicarbonate of soda, which is activated by an acid ingredient (cakes made by this method must go into the oven as soon as the acid ingredient is added). So can these 'chemical' ingredients be left out of a recipe? No, is the simple answer. They're raising agents, and the recipe has been devised to work with their help.

242 Layer cake mix — for 30!

If you're making a layer cake to serve a large gathering, do yourself a favour and use an 'all in one' recipe — you literally mix all the ingredients at once, ideally in a food processor or using a handheld electric mixer. The trick is to use really soft butter to ensure rapid mixing. To make one large cake, you'll need 2 x 30 cm (2 x 12-inch) tins. Scale up the ingredients (a 30 cm/12-inch tin holds roughly twice the volume of a 23 cm/ 9-inch tin or four times the volume of a 15 cm/6-inch tin), and remember to allow extra baking time.

243 Not a moment to improvise

It's important to use the size and type of tin specified in the recipe, or you could end up with a disappointingly flat cake or one with a molten center. It's also important to use the specified ingredients — a dark, thick sugar is no substitute for caster sugar in a light layer cake, for example. As always, make sure your ingredients are fresh and the best quality — unrefined sugar, free-range eggs and good unsalted butter.

FIX IT

Curdling cake? If your layer cake mix starts to curdle when you're adding the eggs, beat in about 1 tablespoon (15 ml) of the flour to rescue the mixture by stabilizing it.

244 Is it done yet?

It's important not to open the oven until the cake is almost baked, as a sudden drop in temperature in the early stages will cause the cake to collapse. Remember there will be some residual cooking after it comes out of the oven, so under-bake rather than overdo it. When the cooking time is almost up, there are several ways to check whether the cake is baked all the way through.

The squeak test Put your ear to the cake (very carefully, of course) — if there's still an audible squeak, it needs a little longer.

The fingertip test Press the centre of the cake very lightly with your fingertip — it should indent then spring back to shape immediately.

The skewer test (see below) Insert a skewer into the centre of the cake, then remove it. It should come out 'clean' — that is, with no trace of uncooked batter.

SUGAR FLAVOUR COMBOS

Infusing a jar of sugar with a flavour is a simple but very effective way to get an intense flavour into your cake or biscuits. Yum! Vanilla and cinnamon sugar are classics, but try the following cake combinations:

Chocolate cake

star anise   sugar

Lemon cake

lavender   sugar

Ginger cake

rosemary   sugar

245 Just a pinch

It might seem odd to add a pinch of salt to a cake, but it adds depth to the flavour. Make sure the 'pinch' is just that — you shouldn't be at all aware of its presence.

DINNER'S AT EIGHT

Whether you're eating alone or serving dinner for six (or more), it's important to introduce a sense of occasion — and where better to start than with a beautifully set table to create atmosphere and anticipation. In this chapter, we explore ways to make your dining space enticing — and how to make the food look great, too.

Set the scene

Highly polished antique mahogany or cheap and chic painted pine, your dining table is the focus of your eating experience, so make it gorgeous and welcoming with a few clever touches.

246 Where does everything go?

Place settings are a simple matter of logic. The conventional layout is a hangover from a time when formal dinners followed an identical progression — soup, fish (served with white wine), meat (with red wine) and so on — but since courses are often skipped or reversed or are more eclectic nowadays, your main aim is not to confuse your guests. However, if your menu and/or the occasion demands it, or you just fancy something different, consider using a formal place setting, as shown below.

Conventional table setting

Small bread plate with a knife for spreading butter.

Arrange glassware with the wine glasses in the order in which they'll be used, from the outside in, and the water glass to the left.

For desserts that require a spoon and fork, arrange the silverware at the top of the place setting, spoon above fork — but if you're serving ice cream in tiny coffee cups, for example, it makes far more sense to place a teaspoon on the saucer when you serve.

Arrange silverware from the outside in, in the order (and hand) in which each piece will be used.

Formal French table setting

No bread plate or butter knife — the bread is placed on the table and eaten without butter.

Arrange glassware in the order in which it'll be used, with smaller glasses in front.

Arrange forks with the tines facing down. From the outside in: fish fork, dinner fork, salad fork.

The fish-course plate sits on top, dinner plate in the middle. Serve salad on a separate plate after removing the dinner and service plates.

Arrange silverware from the outside in, in the order (and hand) in which each piece will be used. Place the soup spoon bowl-down.

TRY IT

Be dramatic! For a really bold look, abandon the conventional china plate in favour of a wooden board or a slab of slate. Slate in particular is a wonderful foil for the striking colours of food; wood has a rather rugged, rustic feel — perfect for rugged, rustic dishes.

247 Make it easy on yourself (and your guests)

When planning what tableware to use, always consider your menu. For example, deep-rimmed bowls are great for fork-only dishes such as risotto, and for strand pasta where it's helpful to brace the spoon against the rim while you twirl the strands with the fork. However, for anything that requires a knife and fork, a flat plate with a shallow rim is far more user-friendly and avoids undignified flying elbows.

248 Napkin folding for the grand occasion (or a touch of irony)

Formal damask napkins, stiff with starch, might be more associated with an upscale restaurant than a family dining room, but they do have one big advantage — you can fold them into amazing shapes and make them a feature of your table setting. At the very least, roll each napkin into a cylinder and secure it with a pretty napkin ring.

FIX IT

Not into napkin folding? If starched linen isn't your thing, look out for vintage tea towels — monogrammed with your initials, if you're lucky — to use as napkins, or make your own from vintage fabric such as grain/seed sacks or ticking. And instead of silver napkin rings, improvise with a strand of ivy in winter, scented honeysuckle in summer or ribbon, raffia or even jute twine. Informal and charming!

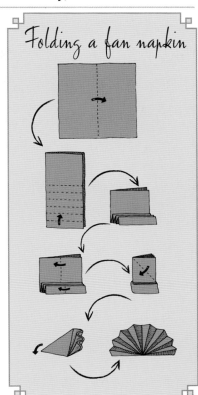

Folding a fan napkin

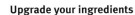
Upgrade your ingredients
Stylish presentation allows you to turn the most humble of ingredients — such as the potato and herb soup shown here — into a spectacular appetizer.

249 Mismatched china

When choosing tableware, you really can't go wrong with plain white. It sets off the food beautifully and unobtrusively, and even inexpensive white tableware looks good. But if you like a bit of colour, gather together a mismatched set of tableware from charity shops. And be bold about it — put side plates with the wrong dinner plates, put cups on the wrong saucers. Pull it together with napkin colours, or flower colours, or food colours — or even the era of food you serve.

250 Have fun with presentation

Devise a menu that allows you to present the food in ways that invite delighted comments. For example, tie thin breadsticks into bundles of three with raffia; serve asparagus alongside soft-boiled eggs in novelty egg cups or miniature zinc buckets; line up three different chilled soups in shot glasses and set your homemade jelly in martini glasses.

251 No candlesticks? Improvise!

Candlelight is a must, and the more, the better — fill every available surface! A candelabra with long, tapering dinner candles makes a striking centrepiece for the table, but glass jars and ramekins are cheap and plentiful and reflect the candlelight (use tea light candles with a generous burn time), producing an abundance of sparkling light. A long row snaking the length of the table looks magical. Glass lends itself to all sorts of decoration, from designs in special glass paint to dried citrus fruit slices tied on with raffia — or simply let it speak for itself.

252 Floral fancies

If you lack a statement candelabra for the centre of the table, use a vase or jug of flowers instead. Match the flowers to the mood of the menu — an elegant arrangement for a formal dinner, wild flowers in a jug for an informal one. Two things to remember — keep the arrangement to a manageable size, so your guests won't have to peer around it to converse, and avoid flowers with too heady a scent, such as lilies, which can be overpowering in close proximity.

253 Gingerbread for themed parties

Gingerbread decorations make everyone smile. Gingerbread is easy to make and very versatile — craft it into any shape you want and it'll fit the bill for your theme. Celebrating a new home? Recreate it in gingerbread! In need of Christmas decorations? Cut star shapes with cookie cutters and brush them with edible gold or edible glitter. Want something romantic for Valentine's Day? Gingerbread hearts — what else!

Ingredients

350 g (12 oz) plain flour
1 tsp bicarbonate of soda
2 tbsp ground ginger
1 tbsp ground cinnamon
½ tsp ground cloves
125 g (4½ oz) unsalted butter
175 g (6 oz) light brown sugar
Grated zest of 1 orange (optional)
4 tbsp (60 ml) molasses
1 egg, beaten

1 Sift the flour, bicarbonate of soda and spices into a large bowl. Rub in the butter until the mixture resembles breadcrumbs, then stir in the sugar and the orange zest, if using.

2 Warm the molasses slightly in a small pan, remove from the heat and stir in the egg. Add to the flour mixture, mix thoroughly and knead until smooth.

3 Roll out the dough on a floured surface to a thickness of 6 mm (¼ inch) and cut into shapes. If you plan to hang the shapes, make a small hole with a skewer for the ribbon, not too close to the edge. If you're making a gingerbread house, cut to shape using a template.

4 Place the shapes on nonstick baking sheets, allowing plenty of room to spread, and bake at 190°C (375°F) for about 10 minutes, until golden. Allow to cool on the baking sheets for 10 minutes, then transfer to a wire rack to cool completely before decorating.

254 Place cards

Place cards are a lovely touch, from a simple folded white card to one that is hand-decorated with a sprig of lavender or fresh herbs, pressed flower petals or leaves, feathers, buttons or even a piece of fruit (see right) — again, this is a good opportunity to enhance the mood of the menu and table setting. And place cards don't have to be made of card — gingerbread men and women with iced names are a quirky alternative (see recipe, above).

Eat with your eyes

There's a saying that you eat first with your eyes, then your nose, then your mouth — and it's true. It's the sight of a plate of food that initially fills you with delight — or disappointment. Here are some tips on inspiring delight.

255 Less can be more

Getting the balance right between satisfying your visual appetite and overwhelming it is a skill in itself. A *cuisine minceur* (a form of French, low-calorie cooking) portion on a large plate looks mean rather than elegant, whereas a huge portion on a small plate is unappealing, so aim to leave just the right amount of 'artistic white space'. Be aware also of the balance between the elements in each course, and avoid one element that dominates the plate, grabbing more attention than the rest. See pages 150–151 for menu ideas.

256

Gorgeous garnishes

A garnish is
an eye-catching
embellishment, not
necessarily intended to
be eaten. A mandoline comes
into its own here for making thin,
uniform strips, which can then be rolled
together to make a rosette. Carved fruits and
vegetables are the ultimate garnish and with imagination,
patience and a few craft tools, there's no limit to creativity.

3 Golden rules

257

Presentation

1 Build your dish vertically as well as horizontally — for example, serve a slice of roast pork belly at a jaunty angle on a heap of white beans, or a pan-fried cod fillet on top of a neat stack of mashed or puréed vegetables, such as cabbage, potato and carrot.

2 The interior design 'rule of three' works on a dinner plate, too — for example, three whole Chantenay carrots look far more harmonious than two or four. Five works, too!

3 Consider colour and texture — monochromatic food with no variation in texture holds very little appeal for the senses. If in doubt, add a few sprigs basil, watercress or some baby rocket leaves. There's very little that's not improved by a splash of green!

258

Swipe, dab, blob, drizzle, trickle, splash

This is where you get creative. Positively 'cheffy', in fact! With a few props, such as a spoon, a paintbrush, a squeeze bottle or an oil pourer, you can dress up a plate and make it as elegant or flamboyant as you like. Have fun with it, but remember that less is more.

Blob Useful for accents, such as fruit coulis — the sort of thing you serve in smaller quantities. Blob from a spoon, or from a squeeze bottle — this gives you more control for a neat, uniform result. Remember the 'rule of three' when blobbing.

Drizzle For herb-infused oils, balsamic vinegar, vinaigrettes, gremolata and more. Drizzle elegantly from a spoon, an oil pourer or a squeeze bottle. If drizzling straight from an ordinary bottle, cover most of the opening with your thumb to control the flow and prevent a deluge.

Swipe The way to give vegetable purées a presence. Place a small spoonful on the plate, place a tablespoon in the centre and swipe into a comma shape. You can also swipe thinner sauces, such as coulis, in a straight line with a paintbrush — think of a strié paint effect.

Here are three classic menus for elegant dining, with white china, sparkling glass and starched napkins. Everything can be prepared in advance, allowing you to be at the table with your guests instead of slaving over a hot stove.

MENU ONE

STARTER
Twice-baked smoked salmon soufflés with watercress microgreens and lemon vinaigrette

MAIN COURSE
Beef Wellington with wilted spinach, steamed green beans and whole baby carrots

DESSERT
Vanilla crème brûlée

MENU TWO

STARTER
Chilled pea, pancetta and mint soup with baby bread rolls

MAIN COURSE
Roast lamb with lavender, gratin dauphinois and broccoli

DESSERT
Orange sorbet with ginger tuiles

MENU THREE

STARTER
Chicken liver pâté with melba toast and rocket

MAIN COURSE
Baked trout with almonds, roasted new potatoes, watercress and fennel salad

DESSERT
Mini Black Forest cakes with cherry compôte

Menu inspirations

If you really want to impress your guests and whet their appetites, print out menus for the occasion and display them on the table, or even send with invites. If that doesn't suit your style, then at the very least conjure one up mentally and use it as a tool to help you visualize the meal as a whole.

260 Presentation skills

These menus allow you to show off your presentation skills. Think through how to make everything look spectacular, no matter how simple the ingredients — for example, make pasta sheets with mint leaves and flowers for the open lasagne and stack slices of belly pork on the beans.

MENU ONE

STARTER
Open prawn and broad bean lasagne

MAIN COURSE
Slow-braised lamb shanks
with Puy lentils and kale

DESSERT
Individual New York cheesecakes with
raspberry coulis and edible flowers

MENU TWO

STARTER
Ravioli stuffed with mushroom duxelles

MAIN COURSE
Pork belly with golden crackling, flageolet
beans and roasted tomatoes

DESSERT
Coconut and lime ice cream

MENU THREE

STARTER
Beetroot carpaccio with feta and microgreens

MAIN COURSE
Linguine with creamy tuna and
mushroom sauce

DESSERT
Chocolate coeur à la crème with
chocolate-dipped strawberries

261 Informal supper

These menus suit supper around the kitchen table, with mismatched china and improvised napkins. You can cook and chat at the same time, your friends can crowd round to admire your culinary prowess — and if anything goes wrong, they'll love you anyway!

MENU ONE

STARTER
Griddled asparagus with soft-boiled duck
eggs and sourdough toast

MAIN COURSE
Pan-fried salmon fillets with white bean mash
and tenderstem broccoli

DESSERT
Apple tarte tatin

MENU TWO

STARTER
Crostini with various toppings
(tapenade, broad bean purée, tomato)

MAIN COURSE
Garlic prawn risotto primavera

DESSERT
Balsamic zabaglione with strawberries

MENU THREE

STARTER
Pear and prosciutto salad with soda bread

MAIN COURSE
Polenta with Gruyère and
creamy tarragon mushrooms

DESSERT
Îles flottantes ('floating islands' — meringues
floating in custard)

262 Buffet for a creative gathering

Any arts and crafts gathering requires a generous supply of nibbles to sustain the creative spirit, so a buffet is perfect — but quilters, knitters and the like also need clean, grease-free hands, so a little fun and ingenuity is called for in the menu. Serve chilled or warm blended soups in shot glasses with garnishes, *arancini* (risotto balls) on cocktail sticks, mini sushi rolls with mini chopsticks, cake/cookie/pie pops on sticks — things that are satisfying but not messy to eat.

- **Chilled soups** Avocado, gazpacho, almond, vichyssoise
- **Warm soups** Beetroot, sweet potato, mushroom, chicken
- **Arancini** Chicken, shrimp, mozzarella, pesto
- **Pie pops** Spinach and feta, chicken and mushroom, butternut squash and blue cheese
- **Sushi** Shrimp and avocado, salmon and asparagus, tuna and cucumber
- **Cake pops** Candy-coat or ice the cake pops in colours and designs to match the theme of the gathering.

263 Wheat-free wonders

Guests with food allergies or intolerances always feel a bit of a nuisance to their hosts, so rather than provide something conspicuously different for your afflicted friend, tailor your whole menu around what he or she *can* eat. Here's a sample wheat-free menu:

Avocado and yoghurt dip with polenta crisps
Cook the polenta in a well-flavoured stock and remember to allow time for it to set for making the crisps. Leave the dip until the last minute – the acidity in yoghurt will help prevent oxidation in the avocado, but why take the risk?

Lemon chicken breast en papillote with quinoa tabbouleh
1 Cook the quinoa a few hours in advance and let it cool, uncovered, in a sieve to dry out thoroughly.
2 Complete the tabbouleh, adding raw baby broad beans and toasted pine nuts to your favourite recipe for extra texture and colour.
3 Massage the chicken breasts with lemon and garlic butter, wrap them in a slice of prosciutto and place on top of your chosen vegetables in their individual parcels. They'll need 25–30 minutes in the oven at 190ºC (375ºF).
4 Serve the chicken breasts in their parcels, with a mound of tabbouleh alongside.

Mont Blanc
Lots of scope for flamboyant presentation here, and if you really want to show off, replace some or all of the cream with homemade mascarpone.

264 Vegans love food, too!

Vegan food requires thought, but put together
a good menu and your guest(s) will really appreciate
it, because contrary to popular belief, vegans are
foodies too! All you need to remember is that vegans
don't eat anything with a face, or that's a product
of anything with a face. Here's a three-course
vegan menu:

Shiitake mushroom and spinach sushi
Use brown sushi rice (see page 50). Sauté the
shiitake mushrooms in light sesame oil with garlic
and drain well. Wilt the chopped spinach and squeeze
dry. *Umeboshi* plums, pickled ginger, wasabi and
soy sauce are all fine as accompaniments — but
no fish sauce.

Puy lentils with griddled aubergine, caramelized red onion and mint gremolata
1 Cook the Puy lentils in a well-flavoured vegetable
stock until tender (add a garlic clove to the stock).
2 Meanwhile, roast wedges of red onion in olive oil
until soft and caramelized, and cook round slices of
aubergine, brushed with olive oil, on a ridged griddle
until soft and golden brown.
3 Drain the lentils and toss in olive oil and a little
red wine vinegar. Season well.
4 To serve, arrange the lentils, aubergine slices and
caramelized onion in deep-rimmed bowls, drizzle
generously with mint gremolata and scatter with
toasted pine nuts.

Avocado mousse
Follow the recipe on page 91, but use agave nectar
or maple syrup to sweeten if necessary, instead of
honey, which is not vegan.

265 Pescatarian pleasures

A pescatarian, or pesco-vegetarian, eats fish and
usually dairy but not meat. This makes it less
challenging than a completely vegetarian diet, but
remember not to use meat-related ingredients such
as stock or gelatine. You can get away with serving
two fishy courses — a shellfish appetizer and a
white fish main.

Prawn and fennel bisque with homemade soda bread (see page 139)
A bisque has a delicate flavour and delectable
velvety texture (make sure yours does!). Time
baking the bread so it comes out of the oven about
an hour before you serve the soup, so it's rested
but still enticingly warm.

Tapenade-crusted fish fillets with olive oil mashed potatoes, roasted tomatoes on the vine and sugar snap peas
1 Make the black olive tapenade in advance to give
the flavours time to develop. Use a pestle and
mortar if you have one, rather than a food
processor, to blend the ingredients to a rough paste
with plenty of texture.
2 Spread a thin layer of tapenade on top of the fish
fillets, sprinkle lightly with fresh white breadcrumbs
and bake in the oven at 180°C (350°F) for 15–20
minutes, depending on the thickness of the fish.
Roast the tomatoes at the same time.
3 Meanwhile, cook the potatoes and mash them
with a well-flavoured extra virgin olive oil.
4 Steam the sugar snap peas while you're plating
up everything else, so they're still very crisp and
bright green when you serve them.

Lemon tart
This is the perfect dessert for a fish-based menu —
crisp pastry with a filling that's sharp to the point
of eye-watering. Serve it chilled, dusted with
icing sugar.

Glossary

Aromatic An ingredient added to enhance the natural aromas of a dish. Aromatics include the 'holy trinity' (mirepoix, etc.) as well as flavourings such as herbs and spices.

Baked blind An unfilled pastry shell made using baking beans to support the crust as it bakes. Great for making a really crisp, melt-in-the-mouth shell for sweet and savoury tarts.

Baking Generally the term associated with the production of home-baked goods such as bread, cakes, biscuits, etc., but in technical terms it's a dry heat method of cooking in which the food is surrounded by hot air, as in an oven.

Baste To moisten foods during cooking with melted fat or by dripping a sauce or liquid to prevent drying and to add flavour. It's what you do to roasting meat.

Béchamel A sauce made by thickening milk with a white roux. It only takes minutes to put together and it makes all sorts of dishes really delicious.

Blanching Briefly and partially cooking a food in boiling water. A very useful technique for preparing a glut of vegetables for the freezer. You can also blanch in hot fat, as in an authentic Spanish tortilla.

Boiling A moist heat cooking method that uses convection to transfer heat from hot liquid to a food (approximately 100°C/212°F). You don't need a thermometer to confirm when a liquid is boiling — the enthusiastic bubbling is a sure indicator.

Cooking medium The air, fat, water or steam in which a food is cooked.

Curdling The separation of milk or milk products or egg mixtures into solid and liquid components. Caused by high heat, overcooking or the presence of acids. Ways to avoid curdling are explained where relevant in the book.

Deglaze To dissolve cooked particles remaining on the bottom of a roasting pan or saucepan with a liquid such as water, wine or stock, which is used as the base of a sauce.

Emulsifier This is an agent that combines readily with both the incompatible ingredients in an emulsion (see below), helping them to combine with each other. Effective emulsifiers include honey (useful in vinaigrettes), lecithin (found in egg yolks) and milled starch-based ingredients such as flour.

Emulsion The union of two incompatible ingredients, such as oil and vinegar. An emulsion is either temporary, such as a vinaigrette, which separates within a short time without the aid of an emulsifier, or permanent, such as mayonnaise. Quite a few cooking techniques are emulsion-based.

Folding in The term for incorporating flour into a cake mix, egg whites into a soufflé, etc. — the last step in the preparation process. Use a metal spoon or a rubber spatula and always fold the lighter ingredient into the heavier mixture, using a cutting motion. It's a very gentle action — having gone to the trouble of creating air, you don't want to bash it out with heavy-handed mixing.

Frying Dry heat cooking method in which foods are cooked in a small amount of hot fat; includes sautéeing, stir-frying and pan-frying.

Infuse To extract the flavour from an agent such as herbs or spices by steeping it in a hot liquid (in which case the flavouring agent is usually discarded), or to add flavour to something by steeping it in liquid (in which case the flavouring liquid is usually retained).

Ingredients The most important element of cooking. Freshness is key, both for flavour and for your health — even cupboard ingredients have a limited shelf life, but it's very easy to forget about their existence for months and even years. Source as many ingredients as possible from local and small-scale suppliers — farmers' markets and artisan producers. You'll not only have really fresh, seasonal produce with a known provenance, but you'll also be supporting small producers in a difficult market. Ideally, buy organic, but if that's not possible or available, at least avoid anything with additives. As a rule, their intentions are not honourable!

Intuition Not a culinary term, but a useful thing to develop when it comes to recipes. If a recipe feels wrong, the chances are it IS wrong – they're not foolproof, and do occasionally contain errors. The more you cook from scratch, the more you'll learn to spot potential for wasted ingredients.

Leavener An ingredient or process that produces or incorporates gases in a baked product to increase volume and provide structure and texture. Can be chemical (baking powder) or mechanical (folding in air in whipped egg whites or cream) or biological (yeast).

Marbling Streaks of fat within meat that make it tender and juicy.

Marinate To soak food in a seasoned liquid (a marinade) to add flavour and tenderize.

Mise en place A French term meaning 'to put in place' — it's the discipline of preparing equipment and ingredients before you start cooking, and it's an excellent habit to acquire. Always read the recipe from start to finish before you start to make sure there are no surprise instructions lurking halfway down. Preheat the oven if relevant, prepare pans or dishes and finally assemble the ingredients and carry out any preparation such as measuring, chopping, grating or whisking.

Parboiling Partially cooking a food in boiling or simmering liquid. It's useful for starting things off and essential for the perfect roast potato.

Pinch A 'pinch' of an ingredient means just that – the amount you can pinch between your forefinger and thumb. The generosity of the pinch depends on personal taste preference.

Poaching A moist heat cooking method that uses convection to transfer heat through submergence in a liquid (approximately 71°C–82°C/160°F–180°F). 'Sous vide' is the new poaching.

Quenelle A snazzy way to serve savoury or sweet mousse, puréed vegetables, whipped cream, ice cream, etc., as a garnish. Scoop the purée (or whatever) from one spoon to an identical spoon until a three-sided oval is formed. A really skilled quenelle-shaper uses only one spoon dipped in hot water, and with a controlled flick of the wrist makes a perfectly smooth egg shape.

Recipe A list of ingredients, placed in the order in which they'll be used, and a step-by-step method, worded unambiguously, to guide you to the finished dish as efficiently as possible. Recipes aren't always this user-friendly, so always read through before starting to cook, to make sure you understand the ingredients and what you're going to do with them, and when.

Residual cooking This is an important consideration when cooking — the residual heat inside food after you've removed it from the hob or oven will continue to cook it. The cooking times given in recipes make allowances for it but it's a process the inexperienced cook needs to learn and trust.

Season to taste Recipes often give the instruction 'Season to taste with salt and pepper' or even just 'Season to taste'. A precise quantity is not given because seasoning is very much a matter of taste. The pepper element is not too difficult, and you'll soon acquire an instinct for how many turns of the pepper mill is just right. Salt is rather more challenging, because there are other elements in the recipe to consider – one that contains Parmesan, for example, will already be salty from the cheese, so proceed with caution. You can put it in but you can't take it out. Recipes often tell you to taste at the end of cooking and 'adjust the seasoning if necessary'. Again, this means mainly salt – you might have added this earlier, but the balance can change during cooking, as some ingredients, such as potatoes, are particularly salt-hungry.

Simmering A moist heat cooking method that uses convection to transfer heat from a hot liquid by submersion (approximately 85°C–96°C/185°F–205°F). Get to know the workings of your hob so you're aware of the point of perfect simmer.

Smoke point The temperature at which a fat begins to break down and smoke. Smoke points vary quite a lot (see page 107).

Steam A moist heat cooking method in which heat is transferred by contact with steam. The very best way to cook vegetables to avoid loss of nutrients, texture and colour.

Tempering The process of adding hot liquid gradually to eggs to stabilize them and prevent curdling, such as when making custard. Once the eggs are safely tempered, you can add the remaining liquid all at once. Give the process a head start by using eggs at room temperature.

Timings The timings given in recipes are for guidance only, as equipment and heat sources vary widely. A good recipe tells you what to expect at each stage — for example, 'sauté the onions for 5 minutes, until soft but not brown' or 'bake for 25–30 minutes, until well risen and golden' — so that if your timings don't exactly correspond with those specified, at least you won't ruin your dish.

Zest The outer rind of citrus fruit, which contains the oil, flavour and aroma. Slightly addictive, so you might find yourself with a lot of bald lemons in the refrigerator.

Reference charts

Chilled food storage

Meat, fish and dairy produce has the potential to spoil very quickly if not stored and cooked properly. The following are the recommended health and safety guidelines for maximum storage times and minimum safe cooking temperatures. Grains and vegetables are less of a health hazard and the cooking times given below are recommended for best results.

Refrigerator		Freezer	
BEEF			
Roasting cuts	Up to 5 days	Up to 1 year	Roasting cuts
Steaks	Up to 5 days	Up to 1 year	Steaks
Mince	Up to 2 days	Up to 4 months	Mince
LAMB			
Roasting cuts	Up to 5 days	Up to 1 year	Roasting cuts
Small cuts (chops, etc.)	Up to 5 days	Up to 6 months	Small cuts (chops, etc.)
Mince	Up to 2 days	Up to 4 months	Mince
PORK			
Roasting and small cuts	Up to 5 days	Up to 1 year	Roasting cuts
Mince	Up to 2 days	Up to 3 months	Mince
Bacon	Up to 7 days	Up to 1 month	Bacon
SAUSAGES			
	Up to 2 days	Up to 2 months	
CHICKEN			
Whole	Up to 7 days	Up to 1 year	Whole
Pieces (breasts, etc.)	Up to 2 days	Up to 4 months	Pieces (breasts, etc.)
LEAN FISH			
	Up to 2 days	Up to 6 months	

Cooking grains

Grain	Liquid (ml)	Cooking (mins)	Resting (mins)
Polenta	vol x 5	45	n/a
Quinoa	vol x 2	15	5
Millet	vol x 3	15	20
Buckwheat	vol x 2	15–20	n/a
Long-grain white rice	vol x 1 ⅓	20	5

Cooking vegetables

Type	Name	Steam (mins)	Boil (mins)	Eat raw?
Root	Carrots	6–8	6–10	Yes
	Parsnips	7–10	8–10	Yes (if young)
	Turnip	8–12	8–15	Yes
	Celeriac	12–15	15–20	Yes
	Beetroot	40–60	30–60	Yes
Tuber	Potatoes	8–12	8–15	No
	Sweet potatoes	7–10	8–10	No
	Jerusalem artichokes	5–8	6–10	Yes

Chilled food storage

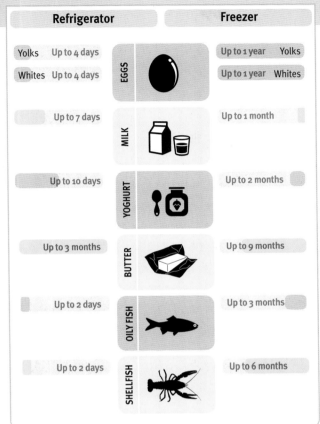

	Refrigerator	Freezer
EGGS	Yolks Up to 4 days Whites Up to 4 days	Up to 1 year Yolks Up to 1 year Whites
MILK	Up to 7 days	Up to 1 month
YOGHURT	Up to 10 days	Up to 2 months
BUTTER	Up to 3 months	Up to 9 months
OILY FISH	Up to 2 days	Up to 3 months
SHELLFISH	Up to 2 days	Up to 6 months

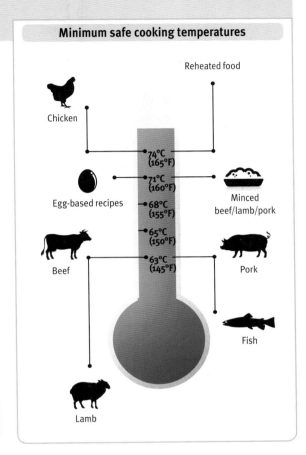

Minimum safe cooking temperatures

- Chicken — 74°C (165°F)
- Reheated food — 74°C (165°F)
- Egg-based recipes — 71°C (160°F)
- Minced beef/lamb/pork — 71°C (160°F)
- 68°C (155°F)
- 65°C (150°F)
- Beef — 63°C (145°F)
- Pork — 63°C (145°F)
- Fish
- Lamb

Cooking vegetables

Type	Name	Steam (mins)	Boil (mins)	Eat raw?	Type	Name	Steam (mins)	Boil (mins)	Eat raw?
Beetroot	Beetroot greens	5–7	5–6	Yes	**Brassica**	Broccoli	4–5	4–6	Yes (best blanched for 2 minutes)
	Spinach	2–4	2–3	Yes		Cauliflower	3–5	4–6	Yes
	Chard	3–5	3–4	Yes		Cabbage	4–6	5–6	Yes
Legume	Green beans	4–6	3–6	Yes (best blanched for 2 minutes)		Kale	4–6	5–6	Yes
	Broad beans	7–12	5–10	Yes (if young)		Brussels sprouts	10–15	10–12	Yes
	Peas	3–5	2–3	Yes (if young)		Pak choi	3–5	3–4	Yes

Index

Credits

Thanks to Viv Brett and Gill Crossley for their help and advice.

Quarto would like to thank the following for supplying images for inclusion in this book:

A Aleksii, Shutterstock.com, p.67
Achmann, Andreas/FC, StockFood UK, p.28
Adamache, Laura, Shutterstock.com, p.139bl
Afanasieva, Olha, Shutterstock.com, p.115
Africa Studio, Shutterstock.com, pp.142–143, 146b
Angorius, Shutterstock.com, p.23t
Annata78, Shutterstock.com, p.25b
Baier, Lacey, p.34bl-r
Black, Ruth, Shutterstock.com, p.118c
Bon Appetit, Alamy, pp.34t, 42cl
Brauner, M., StockFood, p.141tcl
Campbell, Ryla, StockFood UK, p.104
Carriere, James, StockFood, p.24
Chen, Jill, Shutterstock.com, pp.64tl, 140, 153r
Chiyacat, Shutterstock.com, p.120bl
CiprianCB, Shutterstock.com, p.87br
CirclePS, Shutterstock.com, p.63br
Condé Nast Collection, StockFood, p.152l
Cultura Creative Ltd., StockFood UK, p.150–151
De Marco, Francesco, Shutterstock.com, p.32bl
Dinner, Allison, StockFood UK, p.76–77
Dmytro, Sukharevskyy, Shutterstock.com, pp.108–109, 111
Dream79, Shutterstock.com, p.118t
Duncan Loughrey, StockFood UK, p.35bl
Eising Studio — Food Photo & Video, StockFood, pp.30b, 64tr
ElenaKor, Shutterstock.com, p.63tr
Elya, Ezz Mika, Shutterstock.com, p.14–15
Emprize, Shutterstock.com, p.25tr
Eskymaks, Shutterstock.com, p.147t
F. Strauss, StockFood, p.147b
Firmston, Victoria, StockFood UK, p.148
FoodPhotogr. Eising, StockFood UK, pp.50b, 58–59, 122tr/cr/br
Frank, Tatiana, Shutterstock.com, p.66t
Gallo Images Pty Ltd., StockFood, pp.35br, 45
Getty, pp.42cr, 47t, 127b
Gough, Joe, Shutterstock.com, p.39tl
Gourmetphotography, Shutterstock.com, p.125
Gruendemann, Eva, Shutterstock.com, p.128–129
Hamon, J.-F., StockFood UK, p.40l
Holsten/Koops, StockFood UK, p.31

iStockPhoto, p.53b
Johnbraid, Shutterstock.com, p.89
Jost Hiller, StockFood, p.153l
Karl Newedel, StockFood, p.149tl
Keller & Keller Photography, StockFood UK, p.73l
Kristensen, Lasse, Shutterstock.com, p.127t
LilKar, Shutterstock.com, p.85
Lister, Louise, StockFood, p.68l
Loskutnikov, Shutterstock.com, p.101
Louella938, Shutterstock.com, p.38tl
MARCELODLT, Shutterstock.com, p.64br
Margouillat Photo, Shutterstock.com, p.55
Marmo81, Shutterstock.com, p60t
Monkey Business Images, Shutterstock.com, pp.97t, 117r
Monticello, p.44bl
Mosin, Juriah, Shutterstock.com, p.6
Msheldrake, Shutterstock.com, p.123
Mueller, Adrian/FC, StockFood UK, p.13t
Nadolski, Peter, Shutterstock.com, p.119r
Natalia, Lisovskaya, Shutterstock.com, p.54
Nattika, Shutterstock.com, p.131br
Nui7711, Shutterstock.com, p.131bl
Octopus Collection, StockFood UK, pp.43, 134tl/tr/cr
Oldbunyip, Shutterstock.com, p.105br
Paul, Michael, StockFood UK, p.82
Paulista, Shutterstock.com, p.69tr
Photo Africa, Shutterstock.com, p.93tr
PhotoCuisine, pp.2, 29, 32b, 33b, 37, 38tr, 39bl, 40, 44t, 47b, 50, 65, 80, 84t, 86, 91tl, 94, 95bl, 98b, 103b, 107, 113, 124, 131t, 135b, 145r, 149bl, 152r
Picture Box/Luna, StockFood UK, p.30t
Pollak, Katharine, StockFood, p.146t
Pretty Vintage Table, www.prettyvintagetable.com, p.145b
R&R Publications Marketing Pty Ltd., StockFood, p.118b
Rangizzz, Shutterstock.com, p.112
Raths, Alexander, Shutterstock.com, p.16
Ribeiroantonio, Shutterstock.com, p.87
Richard Jung Photography, StockFood UK, p.136l
Rix, Jane, Shutterstock.com, p.22tl
Schieren, Bodo A., StockFood UK, p.62
Schweitzer, Elena, Shutterstock.com, p.48–49
Seagames50, Shutterstock.com, p.66b

Shaw, William, Getty, p.21b
Sherstobitov, Alexander, Shutterstock.com, p.22
Sima, Viorel, Shutterstock.com, p.110t
Slava17, Shutterstock.com, p.120br
Smirnova, Ekaterina, Shutterstock.com, p.93b
Stevemart, Shutterstock.com, p.90bl
StockFood, Cultura, p.8
Stowell, Roger, StockFood, p.23bl
Teerapun, Shutterstock.com, p.51
Tim Hill, Alamy, p.87bl
Velychko, Shutterstock.com, p.57t
Volosina, Shutterstock.com, p.33t
Weaver, Stephanie, StockFood UK, p.133b
YuriyZhuravov, Shutterstock.com, p.32t
Zabert Sandmann Verlag, StockFood, p.26–27
Zogbaum, Armin, StockFood, p.19t

All small reference images on pp.10–11, 12, 17, 21, 25, 28, 41, 51, 54, 60, 65, 67, 72, 81, 82, 85, 88, 91, 95, 97, 101, 113, 114, 115, 121, 127, 135, 140, Shutterstock.com

All step-by-step and other images are the copyright of Quarto Publishing plc. While every effort has been made to credit contributors, Quarto would like to apologize should there have been any omissions or errors, and would be pleased to make the appropriate correction for future editions of the book.